GW00385429

MUCH LOVE
and
GREAT SADNESS

Helen Dolman with her first baby

MUCH LOVE
and
GREAT SADNESS

Memories of a Catholic Lady
of Herefordshire 1810-1851
by
Anne Helen Dolman

Edited with a Foreword
by

N. C. Reeves

Published in 1988
© *Copyright Mrs. E. Snead Cox*
ISBN 085 244 1479

Printed by
Davis Brothers, Leominster, Herefordshire.

CONTENTS

Illustrations

Foreword

Anne Helen Dolman was born in 1810, a daughter of Dr. Samuel Cox of Eaton Bishop, near Hereford. The Coxes were of a devout Catholic family which had managed to preserve its faith and fortune in spite of the penal laws which made this very difficult for Catholics.

Dr. Cox had obtained his M.D. at Glasgow in 1802, and at the time of Helen's birth was practising in Durham. He had a family of ten children, most of whom died young. At the time when Helen was writing her reminiscences, only Clementine, a Visitation nun at Le Mans, and Richard Snead were alive besides herself.

When Dr. Cox eventually returned to Eaton Bishop, he and two of his sons, especially George Duncumbe and Richard Snead, did much to assist in the revival of Catholicism which followed Catholic emancipation in 1829.

It is clear from the surviving papers of the family that all the Coxes were scribblers, but Helen's "Recollections", written in 1872, are especially entertaining and interesting as a picture of Catholic family life in this period of rapid social change. Helen appears in these pages as a most attractive character, and a sensitive and intelligent observer of the stirring events which followed the French Revolution and the abolition of the penal laws against Catholics.

Helen's reminiscences end with the death of her father in 1851, but she lived another forty eventful years. In 1833 she had married John Dolman, a surgeon who qualified at London University, and who, like Helen, was a devout Catholic. After their marriage, he practised in York, where by his charitableness, he came to be known as the "Father of the Poor".

In 1852, the Dolmans retired to the manor of Souldern in Oxfordshire, which had been handed over to them by Richard Snead, Helen's brother, then of Broxwood. When John Dolman died in 1867, Helen left Souldern to Mary Helen, her daughter who had married Brian Stapleton. She herself went to live at St. Mary Hill, near the Dominican Priory at Woodchester. Her son George lived with her until her death and then went to Oscott to train as a priest. Her other son, Marmaduke, was somewhat of a disappointment to his mother, for, in his uncle's words, "He employed his superior talents in fitful and unfruitful labours, injuring no one but himself," dying in 1889, aged fifty.

Helen and her brother, Richard Snead, were always very close, and their children spent much time together.

Helen died, much loved and full of good works, and happy in the lives of her children and their children, in 1891. Richard Snead, writing in his diary on the 23rd December, recorded his last look at the face "of my dear sister, the last remaining to me of our once numerous family". She was buried beside her husband, John, at Hethe, near Souldern.

———————————

Mary Helen Stapleton, besides raising a large family, distinguished herself as a historian, writing a "History of Kidlington", and "The Oxford Mission". Also "A History of the Post-Reformation Catholic Missions in Oxfordshire".

Helen Dolman's brother, Richard Snead Cox, was the builder of Broxwood Court near Kington, Herefordshire. Besides the Court, he built the beautiful church of the Holy Family and a Catholic school in Broxwood.

The present Richard Snead Cox is his great grandson.

Arms of Cox of Broxwood, Souldern and Eaton Bishop

Recollections from 1817
of Anne Helen Dolman
An Autobiography
Childhood and Youth

I have been told that I was born on the 13th November, 1810. The house in which I was first introduced into the world was in Old Elvet Street, Durham, and is now the Presbytery. There was a field in the premises which is now the site of the Catholic Church. In my infantine days, I remember my brother and his boy friend (Tom Constable) hunting some unfortunate pigs with bows and arrows, and I with other little ones was perched upon a wall to be out of harm's way. This sport continued until one unlucky day an arrow transpierced poor piggy, and so put a stop to our fun. In the same street there was a mysterious old house in which my parents had resided before my time, and which had the reputation of being haunted, and was in fact abandoned by them on this account, as no servant would live in it. It was never clearly known what particular Ghost resided there, but certain it is that strange occurrences took place in it; such as footsteps heard on the stairs when no one was about, bells rung at night, the bed curtains drawn and undrawn by invisible hands. Sometimes all the inmates of the house would assemble on one particular landing of the stairs, having been roused from their sleep, and each one thinking that he had been called to that spot. These things happened to sensible, well-educated people, who were not likely to be deluded by fancy. I well remember, as a child, passing the house with a kind of awe, and peeping through the key-hole to see if I could see any Ghosts.

As I left Durham before my 9th birthday my recollection of the place is rather vague, and the dates rather confused, but my earliest recollection goes back to my second year, when I well remember a huge lobster which was brought into the house, so huge that everyone went into the kitchen to see it. I began to tease it with a straw, when it put out its nippers and bit my finger so as nearly to pinch it off.

Many of my mother's friends I remember; among them was Mr. Clavering, a bachelor of the Callaby family, who was much respected by everyone and (generally) went commonly by the name of Billy Clavering.[1] He was very fond of flowers and border trimming; and we children, as we watched him from the nursery window, called him by the irreverent nickname of Billy Border. Another friend was Count Boralaski,[2] commonly called "the little Count"; he was a Polish noble of very small dimensions. He lived at Durham, and all the furniture of his house was made to suit his height. He had been married, and the story was that his wife used to lift him to a penitential seat on a big chimney-piece when they had disagreement. He was always very gentlemanly and polite, and I remember him offering a rose to my mother and telling her to plant it as a cutting, which she did, and it grew into a beautiful tree. He died aged 70 years.

In those days it was the custom for the leading members of the congregation to call on the Priest after Mass and sit with him during his breakfast; in this way my parents went in to see Bishop Smith [3] every Sunday, sometimes taking the children with them; afterwards we were ushered into the presence of Bishop Gibson to kneel down and ask his blessing. He was very old and infirm and had to be wheeled about in an invalid chair. His Coadjutor, Bishop Smith, was a great friend and constant visitor at my father's house; he taught me my Catechism and all about the Passion of Our Lord. When he came to the carriage of the Cross, in my childish mind I connected it with the glittering gold and yellow carriage of the Lord Sheriff (Mr. Lambton) which I had in great admiration, but I could not connect it with Our Blessed Lord's suffering, and I felt puzzled.

We occasionally went to visit the Carmelite nuns at Cocken, a community now settled at Darlington. No sooner was my sister Clementina introduced to them than she made up her mind to join that order; but her health was too delicate and she ultimately

---

1 Billy Clavering - member of the Catholic and Jacobite family of Callaly Castle, Northumberland. William and John Cleavering of Callaly were taken prisoners at Preston in 1715.

2 Count Joseph Boruwlaski was 3ft. 3ins. tall but was well proportioned, and learned and more than ordinarily intelligent. He was popular with Cathedral Clergy and the local gentry. He spent 40 years in Durham and died there in 1837, aged 98. He was buried in the Cathedral. Helen was wrong about his age.

3 Bishop Smith - in 1826, the Jesuits who had hitherto served the mission at Durham, made over the Chapel to Bishop Smith, Vicar Apostolic of the Northern district.

joined the Visitation nuns at Le Mans, France. Just before she paid the visit to Cocken my mother had been teaching her the Catechism and telling her of the pains of hell. She threw her arms around her mother's neck exclaiming. "Oh Mamma, never let me go to that dreadful place". From that time her religious vocation was fixed.

I remember at this time the illuminations for the Battle of Waterloo and how I used to be teased about the young Napoleon, then the same age as myself; he died Duke of Reichstadt, 1830. My father at this time rode a very beautiful horse, a most vicious animal "One day", says Mrs. Salvin,[1] "when I was walking in his grounds with my sister-in-law, Mrs. Riddell, suddenly we saw a gate flying in the air. We rushed to the place to see this strange phenomenon and met my father; he had opened a gate to pass through, when his horse suddenly kicked out behind, lifting the gate completely off its hinges and sending it up to a great distance in the air". The animal was so wicked, he was obliged to be sold. At this time Mrs. Salvin of Croxdale had also a most vicious horse. One day she sent the groom into Durham on a commission; he rode this animal, and, in crossing a bridge over the river, the horse became unmanageable, backed, and threw him into the river Wear, and he was drowned. On one occasion, as a great treat, we were all sent to dine with a family as numerous as ourselves. We had dinner in the nursery and one pigeon was served; and I remember thinking how very small each one's portion would be. About this time an unfortunate letter-carrier was hanged for opening a letter. He melted the sealing-wax with the steam from a kettle. Such was the legal punishment in those days. The scaffold could be seen from our house, and my mother had the blinds all drawn to prevent anyone from looking on; but the house-maid who was very ill in bed with diphtheria, actually got up and, to my mother's intense disgust and indignation, was found looking through an attic window from where she could get a good view of the execution. Mr. and Mrs. McKencer [2] were among my mother's acquaintances. They had nine sons and two daughters.

1 The Selvins were Catholic family living at Croxdale Hall, Durham. Mrs. Selvin died 1864.

2 McKencer - this is Helen's version of Macdonald Kinneir. Sir John (1782-1830). He took his mother's name of Kinneir. He was traveller and diplomatist. He published an account of his travels in Persia, America and Kurdistan (1813-1814).

She was a very little woman, but of strong mind and energy and managed to bring up all her big sons by the strength of her will and energy, and with the help of a leather strap called a Taws, a broad piece of leather cut into several thongs at one end; she always carried this instrument in one pocket and some rags in the other so that when she made any wounds or cut fingers she bound up the injury with the latter whilst she caused a wholesome counter-irritation with the former. In consequence, all her sons turned out well. One became a celebrated traveller in the East, and was knighted; another was Arch-deacon of Winchester. Mrs. McDonald had been an heiress, but her husband, who took the name Kencer became bound for a friend, and his wife's property had to be sold, so the widow was not well off when she died.

A story told of Mrs. McDonald, a lady of invincible courage, is doubtless true. One night she heard a noise in the servant's room and went to find the cause. When she got into the room, not seeing any intruder, she looked under the bed and discovered a man concealed there. She at once seized him by the under-jaw putting her thumb into his mouth; and, whilst she dragged him forth, exclaimed "Coom out Laddie", in broad Scotch. She sent off a servant for the constable and managed to hold her prize until she delivered him into the hands of authority. On one occasion she had a dangerous illness and the Doctor ordered her a blister; when it was proposed, she replied, "I came into the world with a whole skin and I intend to leave it with one; none of your blisters for me".

My parents were frequent visitors at the Bishop's palace, and were very intimate with the prebends and their wives; they often dined with the former, where they met all the country gentry. On one occasion there seems to have been no fish; it was Friday and of course we could not eat meat, so eggs were ordered, but, to the confusion of the hostess, there were no eggs, so we had to dine on vegetables.

At this time the wives of the clergy were very tenacious about their rank and precedence, and I believe it had been proposed that the wives of bishops should take the title of Lady. Dr. Barrington was Bishop of Durham at this time. The revenues were £30,000 per annum; some years after they were reduced to £10,000.

We often interchanged visits with the Stanley Constables, and joined in their walks. One day we were enjoying the afternoon together among the hills. I had wandered off by myself and was busy picking heather when I heard a roar behind me. I looked round and beheld a bull running full speed up the hill after me. I was petrified with fear and could not move. I thought my last hour had come and that in an instant I should be tossed upon those fearful horns. I invoked my Angel Guardian to whom I had a great devotion; I heard a tremendous bellow and, being too frightened to stir, remained fixed to the spot. After some time, all being quiet, I recovered my presence of mind and looked round; there was the bull lying on the ground, apparently dead. I ran back to my companions and we all went together to look at the animal; it had actually broken its neck; in running up the hill snorting in the ground, it had caught its horns in the earth and caused its own death. I always afterwards looked upon this incident as a wonderful protection of my Angel Guardian.

Two of this family died at Durham. The eldest girl called Winifred, from being a most perverse, disagreeable child, full of envy and jealousy, became before her death a perfect saint. Bishop Smith, who attended her on her death-bed and during her long and lingering illness, declared that he had never met with so striking an instance of the power of grace over a naturally bad disposition; she was only 16 when she died. The other was the eldest boy, Charles, who died of water on the brain, aged 9 years. The grandmother, Mrs. McDonald, was a constant visitor, and on the arrival of a guest used to say to her little grandson, "Now Charles, make a boo", she always spoke the broadest Scotch. She was widow to Dr. McDonald, whose family had been ruined in the Stuart cause, the head of the family having been beheaded after the rebellion of 1745. It was recorded that at his execution his head was separated from his body and a beautiful white dove was seen to fly up to Heaven as the soul of the departed patriot. His widow lost her reason and wandered about some wood until she was starved to death.

My mother who was very delicate, fell into a sort of decline at this time and the Doctors decided that her only chance of recovery was to go abroad. Accordingly my father made up his mind to quit his practice of physician and go to France, where my grandfather had settled in a Château near Blois in a village called La Chaussée St. Victor, with the ultimate intention of going on to Tours, which was celebrated for its mild climate.

When I was informed that we were going to France my only idea of the country was a round patch upon the map of Europe called by that name. I had not the slightest idea of its being a country with land, trees, and water. A sale of furniture was decided upon, so that during that time, we children went to stay with some friend, Mrs. Michael Dunn's family. One night we were all roused up from our beds by the alarm of house breaks. In fact, some burglars had succeeded in forcing open a window by climbing up on the roof, but when the house was roused, they absconded. I remember a bleak black form being pointed out to me behind one of the chimneys as the robber who had gone there to hide himself. Our visit here was not a happy one. There was a big unfurnished drawing room in which we were allowed to play; the chimney-piece was an old fashioned, high, carved shelf; and on it were several pieces of old china, put there as curiosities out of our reach. One day, whilst we were playing, a shuttlecock unfortunately fell into a cup and brought it down with a crash. Our consternation was great when Miss Hertley, the governess, came into the room and asked who had done the mischief. I am sorry to say that no one owned up to it; so my brother George, because he was the eldest, was fixed upon as the culprit, and was forthwith taken to Mrs. Dunn. Miss Hertley stated the case, saying that George had told an untruth and urged that my Father should be informed, and due chastisement administered. I do not recollect any result, only that we lived in constant dread of the threat being put into execution, and our brightness and happiness were gone. Whilst there, also, my little sister Euphemia climbed on to a table which she over balanced, and she fell on the floor with the table over her. She was severely cut in the forehead. The gash had to be sewn up, and she always retained the mark.

Before leaving the north we went to York to visit the nuns at the "Bar" Convent; we saw a good deal of Miss Friskita Wiseman, sister of Nicholas, afterwards Cardinal Wiseman. Her Mother had lived in Durham to be near her son at Ushaw.

At last the day of departure arrived. My Father engaged the whole of the Highflyer Coach from Durham to London, both inside and out, not a bit too large for a party of eight, and a great quantity of luggage. All that I remember of London was that the family took lodgings at Portland Place. Whilst we were there, the Princess Charlotte died on the 5th November, 1817. A universal gloom prevailed, and no one spoke of anything else. The barrel-organ men went about playing mournful tunes, and the London fogs only added to the general gloom. A quantity of mourning stuffs were bought, and each child had a double suit of black. I wonder if in these days families would incur such an expense for royalty, especially on the eve of going abroad. My 7th birthday happened on the 13th of the same month, and some days before that event my sister Alicia and I had a great quarrel. She said that a girl of seven ought to be ashamed of I forget what; I said I was not seven, so she declared that I was, as my birhtday was so very near. A very vehement dispute ensued during which the footman came in to put some coal on the fire, and was immediately appealed to as umpire. Having heard the case, he decided that until the birthday had passed I not seven but only six, so I was triumphant. When out for a walk with my cousin, I saw a poor little pick-pocket being taken off to prison, and I realised for the first time what that meant. Then we started again on our journey. The journey to Dover occupied two days, and we slept at Rochester on the way. We sailed for Calais in the "Royal George". The passage only lasting two hours, which was remarkably quick, as there was no steam in those days. When we got on board, my mother settled all her children in their little berths and was saying good night. The vessel gave a toss, and before she could balance herself she fell upon a bottle which she had in her hand. Her face was dreadfully cut and her wrist sprained, so that she had to go the rest of the journey with her arm in a sling.

The only thing that I remember of Calais was the yellow velvet furniture of the Hotel, the huge log fires, the dogs, the large faggots and the bellows, all of which were new to me. We then started for Paris, sleeping at Abbeville on the way. We must have stayed some time at Paris; but all I recollect is the Louvre and the incident that the landlady of the Hotel made a present to my mother of a beautiful "Poularade du Mans" (a fat pullet), which she brought to the carriage door just before we started.

After we left Paris, we travelled towards Blois, spending a night at Etampes and another at Orleans. At the Hotel a woman came into the room offering little articles of ivory for sale. We bought some rosaries and an image of Our Blessed Lady. Our nurse being very inquisitive and anxious to see everything, left her room one evening to look into those adjacent. Having opened the door of one, she walked up to the bed, and to her horror saw a corpse laid out. I think the sight cured her curiosity, at least for a time. At Orleans we stayed at a very large, rambling Hotel which took up three sides of a quadrangle. It was called "Les Trois Rois". On arriving, my father perceived a very large and fierce mastiff chained up. Later on, in the dusk of the evening, when he went to reconnoitre, he asked the hostler if the dog was still chained up. He said, "Le matou est il enchainé", instead of the Mâtin, which latter means a mastiff; the former a tom cat. The Frenchman drew himself up with pompous dignity and replied "Monsieur, les matous sont libres en France"; he seemed to think that liberty even to a tom-cat was a great concession. The next thing I remember was arriving at my Grandfather's château at La Chaussé. It was late and supper had been prepared, and I recollect tasting grapes for the first time. The next morning, the ground was covered with snow and the footprints of some large animal could be seen in it. My brother Robert was full of all sorts of stories of wolves in foreign countries, and told us they were the footprints of wolves and that they were in the habit of getting on each others shoulders until they formed a long ladder; then they broke into the first storey and devoured the inmates. We believed it, and great was our terror when we heard the wind at night, quite expecting the objects of our dread to drag us out of bed. The footprints were really those of a large dog belonging to my Grandfather.

The large forest near Blois were infested with wolves. These animals often came into the village of La Chaussée. I remember an old she-wolf and her cubs taking up their quarters in an old quarry. Another time these animals took possession of a lady's garden in her absence. The mayor of Blois used to offer 5 francs for every wolf's head brought to him.

The inmates of my Grandfather's house were himself and his wife, my cousin Alicia, and my two sisters Elizabeth and Clementina and their servants, which made a full house; for which reason, no doubt, a small house not far off was hired for a nursery for the young people, and we had our meals at the Château. A large bell at the top of the house in a small turrret was rung as a summons. The Christmas holidays of that year were kept very merrily. My Grandmother was fond of promoting fun among the young ones, and was very kind in exerting herself on Twelfth Day. We all drew for characters, and sustained them as well as we could. On Holy Innocents we had great fun, all being dressed in different costumes. The summer of 1818 was a very hot one, and I have never forgotten the beautiful flowers, the butterflies and the humming bees, the quantity of apricots and other fruits. There was a beautiful garden and courtyard in front of it. A large quantity of wine was made there, and in the court there was a large cistern intended for brandy distilling: There was a well in the garden, and subterrânean aqueduct conducted the water of the well to the tañks. I mention this circumstance on account of the great alarm to which it gave occasion. My parents always dined at the Château, and the nurse took care of the children at the cottage. One day she was reading an interesting story to us when suddenly little Mary Ann was missed. She was called and searched for in vain. At last someone looked into the tank and there saw a little shoe floating on the top of the water. Of course, poor nurse was in consternation and went up to inform the Master and Mistress, when, to her great relief, she found the little one safe with her mother. At the Château there were three pretty gardens and a shrubbery, in which was a swing; and in the shade of this beautiful little grove we spent many long hours during the heat of the day. I have never experienced any happiness so great as that of those days among the pompom roses and other delicious flowers.

The Curé, Monsieur l'Abbé Besson, was a most frequent visitor at the house; he was a most excellent man, the very model of what a Parish Priest ought to be. There were 500 people in his parish and they looked up to him as a father, and consulted and followed his advice on all occasions; he had been so long at his post that nearly all his flock had been baptized and married by him. No case of immorality had been known in the village for more than 30 years. Monsieur and Madame de Mazancourt were very intimate friends of the family. He was a French Marquis, and his wife a Prussian Countess, very charming people: Before the revolution of 1794 Monsieur had been connected with the Court of Louis 16th and in consequence had lost all his property.

They resided in a very pretty cottage with one servant. Monsieur cultivated the garden, cut up the wood for the fire, and groomed his wife's donkey. No one, to see his delicate hands, could suspect him of such work. He spent much time with my father playing at chess, for he was an excellent player. Some years after, Madame went on a visit to her father, Count Hassan, and there she ruptured a blood vessel and died, leaving her husband to return to France, a broken-hearted widower.

There was a family of the name of Claireveau, who were the principal people of the place, and whom we visited. It consisted of Monsieur and Madame de Claireveau, their daughter Madame Guerin and her daughter MIle Guerin. The former had been very handsome in her younger days: and to save her father from the Guillotine in the reign of terror, had consented to be honoured as the goddess of Reason, and placed on the High Altar of the Cathedral to receive incense. She never ceased to bewail her sin, which was of weakness, not of malice. Her daughter was married to a man to whom she was a stranger, according to the custom of the time; her parents had made up the match and the young people met at the Altar for the first time; the marriage proved an unhappy one, and they separated.

In the year 1818 we all removed into another house. The following May my mother increased her family by a third son and tenth child and he was christened Victor Samuel. The little innocent died at the end of a fortnight. I saw the body before the coffin was closed; it was a beautiful little creature with formed and aristocratic features. A profusion of rosemary was burnt in the room where he lay. He had a Leaden Coffin besides two others, an unknown thing in those parts. On the day of the funeral the body was placed in the hall, four little boys bore it to the grave; the coffin was supported in a sheet carried by the four corners by the boys. In going down the steps leading to the Court, one of the bearers let go his hold and the coffin fell to the ground with a loud hollow sound which roused my poor mother, ill in bed. The children mourners all had crowns of flowers and bouquets for the occasion. My brother was interred in the village church-yard, and many years after, the old Curé was buried in the adjoining grave.

We spent two very happy years in this house full of our games and childish frolics. We were mostly with one nurse, as my mother was often ill, and my father used to spend his time with her, except in the evenings, when he used to read aloud to us. It was our great delight afterwards to act these stories in a long avenue. On the 14th September 1820, the feast of the Exaltation of the Cross, we had just come from Mass when one of the servants came to me and said,

"Your mother wants to speak to you in her room". I obeyed the summons, and entering the room I saw a strange old woman sitting by the fire with a flannel bundle in her lap, which I at once perceived to be a baby. I felt very proud, but was indignant at the intruder, and pretended to see nothing. I went up to the bed and asked my mother if she had sent for me, "Yes, she said, "I want to show you your new brother, after which, he was introduced to me. The Christening took place the following day in the Church. He received the name of Richard.

It was a grand festival; all the villagers were assembled, the bells rang, guns were fired and large quantities of sugar plums and money were thrown up in the air and descended in showers on the the heads of the people, and there was a general scramble. One little boy got his head cut open, which shocked me very much.

In the village of La Chaussée there resided an interesting old man - an English hermit. He lived in a pretty cottage surrounded by a beautiful garden in which he grew fruit trees of every kind, surrounded by a wall and shut in by large green gates. It was a strange coincidence that the family of that man lived in Herefordshire, in the same parish as my grandfather. He was an only son; his parents died whilst he was still young; he joined the British Navy and was taken prisoner with others at Verdun where he remained till all were set at liberty. He inherited an independent fortune from his parents, but had been shamefully robbed of everything by his Trustee, and never obtained any redress, only having sufficient to buy his little property at La Chaussée. He lived on the produce of his garden, having an old woman sometimes to settle up his house for him. He was very generous and always ladened us with fruit and walnuts when we went to see him. My father was very kind to him and often made him presents in money, which was difficult, as he was very proud and sensitive. My mother often attended to his wardrobe, but he as often mended his own clothes; he was model of cleanliness, and all he possessed was in good order. He had a beautiful collection of choice books, maps, and astronomical instruments. He had been a very handsome man, but at this time was worn to a skeleton; he generally wore a suit of white linen. After my parents went to live at Blois, poor Mr. Marsham missed their kind attention, as with increase of age, he became more infirm; so my father took a small house for him adjoining his own. One of the family went to see him every day; it was generally my brother George. One day he perceived a most extraordinary smell which seemed to come from Mr. Marsham's room; on opening the door a dense smoke rushed out and it was with difficulty that he groped his way in. At last he found the corpse of the poor old man lying across the hearth, one side was quite charred, but he still lived and was conscious, but could give no account of the accident - he died a few hours after, as he had lived, being quite ignorant of any religion.

During our residence at La Chaussée a certain English Gentleman, Captain Coluhouse, called on my mother; I believe he was a relative of hers, and had been in her father's regiment at St. Vincent's at the time when he was killed. He gave a circumstantial account of the sad event, by which it was discovered that Captain McLean, my grandfather, although struck down in the morning whilst leading a fragment of the army, did not really die till the evening. When he was disabled, his men carried him into a wood; a carib* passed by the spot, and seeing him still alive, dispatched him. At the time of his death, he appeared to his family in Scotland and stood behind the chair of his daughter (my mother), then a young girl. He was seen by every one in the room, and one of his sisters exclaimed, "Oh! Murdock", and then fainted from the shock. It had often been thought singular that the apparition should not be seen till the evening, when he was supposed to have been slain about 9 o'clock in the morning, at which hour the engagement took place, but Captain Coluhouse explained the mystery when he said that his friend had lingered for several hours in the wood after his men were pursued by the enemy.

In the summer of 1820, my father decided upon leaving La Chaussée, and took a house at Blois. I remember how interested the old Curé was in the matter, and that he seemed particularly impressed by the necessity of a good poultry yard. When a house was chosen and he was told of it, he at once asked my mother "Madame y-a-t'il une basse court pour les poules"? We used to attend the Catechism class at the Cathedral, the boys going to the Abbé Dinan, and the girls to the Abbé Morissat. My brother George and I were the closest friends, and we always went to Church hand-in-hand. We made our 1st Communion together on Corpus Christi, in the company of many hundreds of children. We

---

*carib: a South American Indian

had been in retreat 3 days before, and on the day itself all were dressed in white and each carried a wax candle; mine and George's were of the first class, each weighing one pound. In the afternoon we all went in procession to the font to renew our baptismal vows. The whole ceremony of the day was so impressive that to this day I cannot hear the "Lauda Sion" sung without the deepest emotion, especially that verse "Ecce panis Angelorum".

After the High Mass at which we made our 1st Com, we all left the Church. My mother and sisters met me at the door, and I was so overcome that I fainted.

We had a boy and a girl from the foundling hospital to spend the day with us. Our drawing master's name was Hebour; he was German and had been one of the guards of the Tuillerios when Louis 16th was taken prisoner, and later was placed as sentinel over Charlotte Corday,* before her execution; he was kind to her and she gave him a lock of hair which he always kept as a treasure; he had taken her portrait which hung in his room. Our dancing master was Monsieur Lahouse, and our music master, Monsieur Bonnet, organist at the Cathedral, and a great musical genius. He was considered to be mad during his life, but after his death, his musical compositions were much thought of; he had lived before his time and was not appreciated.

My brother Robert, who was ten years my senior, was much attached to me; he used to call me "nan" and would come to me for anything when my mother was away. In the year 1822, about the month of May, my father and mother heard of his serious illness. He had gone to Worcester after leaving the Jesuit College of St. Acheul, to study the law under Mr. Saunders, the father of Mrs. Hornyold of Blackmore Park. About Easter time he caught a cold which he neglected; it settled on his lungs and ultimately turned to rapid consumption. When my parents arrived at Worcester they found him so ill that they resolved to take him to the South of France, and in due course set off on their journey, intending to take very short stages, and rest frequently on the way. Their first stage was at Evesham about 12 miles from Worcester. I don't know how long they were there, but one day, after taking Robert out in a bath-chair, they returned to the hotel and placed him on a sofa to rest, whilst they sat down to dine in another part of the room. Suddenly my brother was seized with a fit of coughing and expired. My mother, thinking that he had fainted, ran out of the room to fetch

---

* Charlotte Corday, horrified by the blood-thirstiness of Marat, one of the revolutionary leaders, went to Paris and stabbed him in his bath. She was guillotined in 1793.

a restorative, and when she returned, my father made a sign by which she understood that all was over. My father then took up the body of his much beloved son and carried it upstairs, not allowing any stranger to touch it. He was buried at Evesham near the Abbot's tower. An Epitaph was carved upon his tomb-stone, composed by a friend.

"If all that is beautiful, talented and good can draw from the stranger one tear of pity and regret, then tears will be shed on this tomb. Aged 20 years 1822".

My own recollection of Robert is that he was a very handsome youth with curly hair of a bright chestnut colour with blue eyes and a very joyous expression - he was very good-natured and loved his sisters.

When my parents had left for Blois on their way to England, they had given the charge of the family to my sister Clementina who fell dangerously ill of pleurisy, and her life was despaired of. During that time, our innumerable friends were unremitting in their attention to us. The disease ran its course and one day, after many sleepless nights, Clementina fell into a deep slumber, so that the nurse, Madame L'Ami, thought for a moment she was dead. During that sleep she had the following dream: She thought her Angel Guardian appeared to her; he took her by the hand and led her through steep, rugged paths, through briars and thorn till she became very weary; the Angel encouraged her to go on: at last they came to a beautiful place on which was a Temple, she saw the interior of the Temple, and was made to understand that it was the abode of the Blessed Trinity and she knew that the throne of God was there. At the foot of the throne there knelt a young man with folded arms and quite resplendent. The Angel said, "Look again" and she recogonised her brother Robert, and the Angel said "That is your brother praying for you". She then woke feeling refreshed, and the next day she related the dream to Madame Mazancourt, who came to see her daily, and she felt convinced in her own mind that Robert was dead. Clementina began to recover, and when she was strong enough, she sat in an easy chair. One evening she was reading when her nurse had left. The bedroom was unconnected with the rest of the house, being a room of the next house, a door of communication having been opened into the passage of our house. On this special evening my sister was reading when she heard footsteps coming along the passage and stop at her door; she thought it was the nurse, and looked up, expecting to see the door open; however, it remained shut, but the footsteps approached her, and she heard the sound of breathing close to her, but she saw nothing; after a time the sounds seemed to recede and pass into the dressing room, she was seized with great awe, and felt that her brother was dead. When Clementina was ill, the doctor had written to my father to tell him of her extreme danger; his letter seems to have reached its destination at the time of Robert's death; therefore for fear of giving a shock to my sister, my father did not communicate this sad news at home, but merely wrote to say what time we were to expect him at Blois. In fact, we had no idea that Robert had been dangerously ill, much less that he was dead, and we even prepared his bedroom expecting him to return with our parents, and we were in the greatest delight at the thought of having him home again. At last, one Sunday morning my sister Clem, feeling much stronger, ventured to a low Mass at the Carmelite Chapel which was near, and during her absence my parents returned. Their first enquiry was for Clem, the servant said she had gone to Mass; they, knowing how ill she had been, thought she was dead, and that the girl was not speaking the truth. Soon after, we returned, and a sad meeting it was. We did not perceive at first the deep mourning my parents wore, and, not seeing Robert, I ran up into his room expecting to find him there. All the day we were in suspense, not daring to ask any questions. In the evening we heard poor Clem in hysterics, and concluded that something dreadful must have happened. It was only by degrees that we found out the truth, but my mother never mentioned the subject.

During this summer I was asked to "quête"(to ask alms) in the Cathedral for the poor, holding a silver dish. I was dressed in full evening dress. On the morning of the day, the Swiss* came to escort me to the Cathedral, a maid accompanying me. The functionary was dressed in military costume, with cocked hat and plume, carrying his formidable halberd. When making the round I was preceded by the Swiss, who cleared the way. I was muich flattered on hearing some one say, "Elle est jolie comme un ange", and my collection was double in amount, probably because I was "Une petite Anglaise".

When Alicia was at school, she became much attached to one

---

*Swisse - (roughly) "beadle"

of her companions, Felicité. The two friends made a mutual promise that the one who died first would pray for the survivor, who pledged herself to say the Office of the Dead 100 times for the repose of her soul. Some years after that, when the two girls had left school, their friendship cooled to the extent that they did not correspond, and consequently Alicia knew very little of her former friend. One day she was sitting in her room, when suddenly she heard herself called by name, and she at once recognised the voice of her friend Felicité, and became so convinced that she was dead, and had come to claim her promise, that she wrote to enquire about her, and found that she had died on this very day. Of course she fulfilled her promise.

The school to which we were sent was kept by two old ladies, Nuns of the Abbey of Le Lys which had been founded by Queen Blanche, mother of St. Louis. No lady could be admitted unless of the nobility. In the revolution of 1794, the Convent was seized by the "Sans Culottes", and the religious were all dragged to the scaffold and guillotined one after the other. When all but two had been executed a sudden uproar in the crowd announced the arrest of a celebrated aristocrat, and dispersed the mob in pursuit of fresh prey, leaving the two victims awaiting their fate; perceiving themselves to be alone, they ventured to look round, and walked away. They wandered about till they reached Blois, after hiding in the day time, and sometimes begging. When they arrived at that town, the only property they possessed was a silver fork and spoon, on which they borrowed money. The gentry of the neighbourhood who still remained in the country took care of them; and when the heat of the revolution was over they established a secret school for the daughters of "La Noblesse". My five sisters and myself were all at this school at different times. We were the only English girls that the school ever had, and the "Ladies" entertained the greatest affection for us. The establishment was conducted upon anti-revolutionary principles, great form and state being observed. One of the ladies, Madame Sophie de Vouvre was of one of the oldest families in France, and took charge of the school. The other one, Madame Fair, took charge of the house. Madame Vouvre sat in a raised chair which was placed on a dais and railed off from the rest of the school-room like the sanctuary in a church. The strictest etiquette was maintained; and Madame, who was seldom absent from the throne, was held in great awe by the young ladies. The lessons were given by hired masters and mistresses. The uniform was of black silk and included black velvet head-dress, called a "toque", over which, for going out, we wore a long black veil which reached to the knees, made of gauze; there was also a long, detached train to be worn on grand occasions, which was tied round the waist like a court train. On week-days our dresses were of raw silk and Lyon's silk on Sundays. You may wonder how we got introduced to this school, as we were not of the "noblesse francaise". It was this way. My Grandfather had intended to take up his abode at Tours, making only a temporary residence at Blois, but when there, he discovered that the Prefet Mr. Pelet and the Mayor M. Chanvelin had both met him in England, when émigrés took refuge there, and these gentlemen had received attention from my grandfather. They therefore persuaded him to remain at Blois, and introduced us to the noblesse of Blois. There were two other brothers also whom he had met in England, and who supported themselves there by making gold chains. When they emigrated to England one gold coin was all they possessed but, being very ingenious, they beat out the piece and converted it into a chain; this they sold at a profit and made more which they disposed of, and by this means they contrived to support themselves until they returned to their own country. At the Prefecture of Blois a ball was given every month and occasionally my parents attended with one of their daughters. My eldest sister, Elizabeth, was considered very beautiful and was much admired at these balls. Clementina went once and then Alicia came next. One night an English Gentleman came to my father and said, "Where do you keep all your beautiful daughters? No one ever sees them until they are introduced here, one by one"!

Clementina was generally ill, the real cause being her desire to join the nuns of the Visitation at Le Mans. My parents did not object to her being a nun, but only wanted her to stay with them till she was 25; she was then 19. She had intended to join the Carmelites, and had spoken to the Superior at Blois, but she said that her health was too delicate. She had then no intention of being a Visitation Nun; but one night she dreamt that she saw the general resurrection, and herself dressed as a Visitation Nun rising from the grave between the two Sisters de Clanchy, nuns of the Visitation. At the time I write this, these sisters, who were for many years alternately superiors of their Community, have a long time been dead and buried at Le Mans, and it so happened that when my sister Clementina died, her place in the Cemetery was between these two Nuns. After this dream Clementina decided to go to the Convent as soon as she could, and my grandmother encouraged her in her wish. Some pious friends conceived the idea that she was persecuted by my father, who would not allow her to follow her vocation. They requested the Bishop, Monseigneur de Sansanne to call upon my father to remonstrate with him. The Bishop did call, and was shown into the drawingroom, where he found my mother surrounded by her little ones, and she herself very unwell. He paid his visit and returned without naming the subject he had called about. Afterwards the persons who had begged him to interfere asked him if he had called and what had been the result; he replied that he had, and when he saw my mother, he came to the conclusion that the best thing that her daughter could do would be to remain with her and help her. However, my grand-parents had arranged everything, and my parents gave their consent. My Aunt Helen had also offered to take charge of me, being her God-Child, so it was decided that we should leave with my grand-parents who were going to live in Boulogne. Accordingly, in October, we started off with Clementina as far as Le Mans. On our arrival, we took her to the Convent of the Visitation, and she was admitted into the enclosure while we remained at the parlour. She joined the Nuns at supper, after which, she came to see us at the gate, and seemed in very low spirits, and I believe at that moment she felt some regret at the step she had taken, for she told us of some unkind remark the Nuns had made upon the supposed elegance of her dress.

I do not remember anything about our departure from Le Mans except that we had post-horses, and travelled through a cross-country and in passing through a forest one of the horses dropped down dead in the middle of the night. We were in great dread of Banditti and fancied we heard a whistle! but by some means we managed to get to a place called Bernais and put up at a wayside inn for the remainder of the night. There was no accommodation except in one sitting room, and in that we all crowded, and lay down on the floor to rest until daylight, when fresh horses were procured, and then we proceeded on our journey. The next stay was at Montreuil, and then Boulogne. We went to live in a large house in the rue Crebillac, opposite to the Rue de I'Hôpital in which was situated the school of Madame Bruillac, to which afterwards I went as a day scholar.

About this time the engagement between my sister Elizabeth and her cousin was renewed. Seven years before that, my sister, being a very beautiful girl of the Madonna type, very fair with very soft blue eyes, and perfect in form and in manner, was the admiration of all who knew her. She was only 17 when she became acquainted with her father's cousin Samuel. He was rather older than her father and extremely handsome and learned. He undertook to teach her Italian and the consequence was that they became deeply attached, and a mutual promise of marriage was given. All the family objected strongly to the match, on account of relationship and disparity of age. In 1824, a mission was given at Blois by six missioners, all of whom in after life became Bishops, Archbishops and Cardinals. Elizabeth took great interest in the sermons and other exercises. She made a general confession to Monsieur de Fêtre, afterwards Archbishop of Tours; she became totally changed after that, and left off all her finery, took to dressing very plainly, and wished to become a Nun. She mentioned her intention to her director, at the same time telling him of her engagement, and he said that she ought not to break her promise without some very strong reason, and tried to persuade her; but other friends prevailed, and she wrote to her intended to acquaint him of her resolve. When he received her letter, he was so thunderstruck, that he fell down in a faint and was never after like the same man. It was soon after this mission that we all left Blois. Poor cousin Sam was in despair at Elizabeth's refusal, and soon after we got to Boulogne, he sent his brother to try and induce her to change her mind. He succeeded, and wrote to tell his brother of his success, and Sam came at once from England to see her. At last after many lover's quarrels the marriage was fixed for the following April, the relations giving a very reluctant consent. Elizabeth was taken to her cousin's house in London, her grandparents not wishing the wedding to take place from their house. The Cousins were the only attendants at the marriage ceremony, which took place at Father Scott's S. J. Chapel, London. Poor Sam's mind had been so shaken by her refusal that when he actually got possession of his prize, he became outrageously jealous, so much so, that he was insane on the point. He had always been very eccentric but after the wedding all seemed to centre on one point. Poor Elizabeth's life was wretched. After a very short time, her father-in-law and his daughter insisted on taking her to live with them, and the following summer, whilst Sam was absent on business, my grandmother went from Boulogne to fetch her home from London. When her husband returned and found what had been done, he was furious. He did not follow her, but they kept up a correspondence. In the winter 1827, he came to see her and stayed for several months, making himself as disagreeable as possible and behaving very badly to her. Dear Elizabeth was deeply attached to her husband, and she felt his unjust treatment most deeply, when he was present. And when he was away, she grieved so much that she was quite heart-broken. She never spoke to anyone but used to pass her days in reading and working tapestry or in spinning; she was taught the latter by an old woman, and she had a pretty little mahogany wheel made. Things were so uncomfortable that at last Sam returned to London, and in the month of March Elizabeth had an illness which terminated in a rupture of the heart. She continued to get worse during the summer. When her husband heard how ill she was, he came to Boulogne to see her, but she had become so nervous, and the palpitations of the heart so violent, that the doctors said any sudden excitement might cause immediate death. My father, who had come to see her, was of the same opinion as the other doctors; therefore her husband was not allowed to see her, and she was not told of his visit. He had to return to England without seeing her and was very angry. When Autumn came round and she did not recover, it was thought advisable to try the climate of Bath, as she had a great wish to go there. Like most people in her complaint, she took the greatest interest in dress, and had all kinds of new things made in the way of millinery, furs, dresses and jewellry, always remarking when a new thing came from the shop. "This will do for my sister if I do not live to wear it". At last the day of departure was fixed, and we all set sail for England. The party consisted of seven, my father being of the number. My sister was laid on a mattress in the cabin and, being so beautiful, was the admiration of all. She bore the journey very well. We spent one night at Dover and the next at Canterbury, the third at Rochester and the fourth in London.

Cousin Sam met us at the door of the carriage, and lifted his wife into the house; then carried her upstairs to her bedroom. The next day Elizabeth rested, and Sam came to see her. On the following day he did not come, and on the third day, when Elizabeth saw him, she asked why he had not been. Then he asked her why she refused to see him when he was at Boulogne. She answered that she had not known that he was there. He was much surprised, and could scarcely believe that she heard of his visit then for the first time. In the afternoon of that day my uncle called and took Elizabeth and my grandmother out for a drive. On returning, we received them at the door, and Elizabeth was carried upstairs. She had not been two minutes in the room when she made an exclamation and fell back. I lifted her on to her bed, and she was seized with a violent palpitation and seemed to be suffocating, and became terribly excited. A doctor was at once sent for and our French servant at once despatched for a priest. He went for Mr. Wild, an old friend of the family, but he was not at home, and the the servant, not knowing London at all, and only speaking broken English, did not know what to do. At last he contrived to make someone understand that he wanted a Catholic Priest, and he was directed to Father Scott, whom he brought back to the house. The Priest had no idea who had sent for him till he arrived, and to his astonishment, he discovered that the sick person was my sister, whom he had married to her cousin 3 years before; he was also an old friend of the family, and was very much distressed when he heard how the case was. In the meantime the doctor had seen my poor sister. He prescribed something to be taken at once saying, "If that does not restore, be prepared for the worst". of course, he knew that she was dying, and only said that to break the sad intelligence. After the doctor left, we all quitted the room and left her alone with the Priest; she made her confession and received Holy Viaticum all alone, for we had not been told that we might enter the room. The Priest told us after, how much struck he had been by her composure.

She had great difficulty in swallowing the sacred particle, and the Priest gave her a little water which she took without any help. When we all re-entered the room, the Priest began to read the prayers for a departing soul; all present were in such grief that no one could answer them but Elizabeth herself, and she spoke in a loud distinct voice with the greatest composure. From the time of the first attack until she expired was about three hours. She exclaimed "How long it is to die", and the Priest replied, "Remember my dear child that our Lord hung upon the Cross for three hours before he died", and she answered "O yes", and kissing the crucifix with great fervour expired. Before the Doctor came, poor Sam arrived in great distress. He could not believe that Elizabeth was dying and went to purchase a bottle of smelling salts to try and revive her from what he thought was a fainting fit. In the afternoon he came up to the bed-side, where I was, and asked me to retire, and whispered something in her ear. She at once jumped up in bed threw her arms round his neck, kissed him and exclaimed, "Oh Yes!" I think he must have asked her to forgive his unkindness to her. he was heart-broken and sat up all night with the corpse, appearing in great grief. From that day till his death he was never known to mention her name, though he survived for 24 years. He gave poor Elizabeth a most handsome funeral. She died upon her birthday, aged 27.

Now to return to my own life. My grandfather had changed houses, and lived in the high town in the Rue St. Jean when poor Elizabeth rejoined the family. In May of this year I went as a boarder to the Ursuline Convent. It was Rogation Monday, and for the first time in my life, I slept out of my relation's home. I felt very desolate, and everything struck me as being terribly gloomy. The next morning we were called at 5.30 and in due time went to Mass. I felt dreadfully unwell and sat down at the Consecration of the Mass. The Nun behind me, probably thinking that I knew no better, gave me a terrible thump behind my shoulders, which made me kneel down, and the next moment I fainted quite senseless on the floor. When I came to myself two Nuns were making me walk up and down a courtyard, and I never forgot the painful feeling of being forced to walk in that state. By degrees, I got accustomed to the strange ways, and ended up being very attached to the Nuns. Being more delicate than the other girls, the Nuns were very kind in looking after me, But I found it very hard to get accustomed to the cold. We used to have our drawing lessons in a long gallery which was bitterly cold, in winter, and one day my fingers became quite useless from the cold, and the intense pain made me cry. I was sent back to the school-room, and I never forgot the kindness of one of my companions, who, seeing me, exclaimed, "La pauvre enfant, elle a l'onglée dans les doigts", and she put my fingers into her mouth and sucked them until the circulation came back. My great school friends were Catherine O'Connor, cousin of the O'Connor Dow of that day, and Mary Tudor. The former remained in the world unmarried and the latter became a Nun at this Convent, and became blind. We three were always called "Les trois têtes dans un bonnet". This school had a very good reputation; the studies were carried on, on the same principle as the Collège, and we were examined by the same professors. We were about 50 pupils of very mixed classes from the noblesse down to low tradesmens's daughters, and of all countries. The penances principally consisted in learning long lessons, writing verses, kissing the floor, and, for grave faults, keeping one's room, and begging public penance. One very sensational scene occurred whilst I was there. A very beautiful English girl named Walter, one of the pupils, was very ignorant and very stupid for her age. She had been in an English boarding school where she had imbibed many bad habits, and seemed to think of nothing but admiration. She was in poor circumstances. Her father was dead. and her brother had undertaken to have her educated as a governesss, and with that intention she had been sent to the Convent. The poor girl's ignorance and stupidity combined led her into many scrapes, so she resolved to commit suicide. One night she took a cake of vermilion out of her paint box, and when she was in bed, she sucked it. The next morning her face and sheets were in a shocking state; at first she looked as if her throat was cut, but she confessed what she had done. The whole school was summoned and drawn up in two lines at each side of the dormitory, and the culprit was led out of her room by the superior and the general mistress, and had to kneel down and beg public pardon for the scandal she had given. She was excluded from the other children until her friends could be sent for from England, and she was sent home without any of her companions having seen her. In September I went for the holidays to a pretty Château that my father had taken at St. Martin Choquel, about 16 miles from Boulogne. No particular incident happened there, and I returned to school in October. Once a month I used to go home, and various friends of the family came to see me. Among others was Monseigneur L'Abbé Naffree, who spoke English very badly. He was always very proud of any presents given to him, and one day he brought a lace "Alb", beautifully worked. After we had duly admired it, we put it down, but he was not satisfied that we had done justice to it, and exclaimed "But look at the breeches", at the same time pointing to the sleeves. Of course we were much amused. My grandfather had hired a very pretty detached garden at the outskirts of the town; it had a very pretty cottage in it where we used to meet our friends for afternoon tea. It was close to the Castle Walls, and part of the moat was in it. There were very deep sloping banks which were utilised as strawberry beds. Frogs of enormous size abounded, and used to leap as high as my head. I held them ıin the greatest horror. One afternoon, when several people were there, a young gentleman friend made a most beautiful bouquet of roses, which he very prettily handed to me, pointing out a rose in the middle of peculiar fragrance. I put my nose close to it to smell it, when it came in contact with an enormous frog. I was panic-stricken, threw the flowers away with a terrific shriek, took to my heels, and never stopped till I got home, when I was seized with an hysteric fit. To this day I never conquered the dread I got from those creatures, owing to the shock.

At that time we had an old French servant called Blondin who had formerly lived with a very rich Marquise, an eccentric character. Among numerous oddities, one was to have two service of plate, one for meat days the other meagre.* After her death, Blondin lived on his own means in a pretty cottage. My grandfather wanted a trustworthy servant to attend on him, as he was blind, so Blondin, being willing to come, was engaged. He still owned his cottage, which was not far from our house. One day as I was home from school, I took it into my head to dress up like a nun, and for a freak, I ran over to Blondin's to see if he would recognise me. In coming out of his garden, I met three grave ecclesiastics who all took their hats off to me, bowing with profound respect nearly to the ground. One of them was Monseigneur Lariquet, the President of St. Acheul; the others were canons of Arras Cathedral. Not knowing what order I belonged to, they went on to Blondin's to inquire where I came from. He laughed, and said "Oh! that is Madame Cox's Grand-daughter". The clerical gentlemen were very angry, and one of them wrote a strong letter to my grandmother to remonstrate with her for allowing such a profanation, and I got a very severe scolding for my folly.

Among our many friends at Boulogne was a Mr. & Mrs. Tuite. She was a Miss Beaumont of Whitley Abbey. She was a very charming person, and much attached to my poor sister Elizabeth. She had not seen her for sometime, and, calling one day, she was quite shocked to find her so altered, and burst into tears. We who were living with her had not noticed the change. Mrs. Tuite, who died about two years after Elizabeth, had an extraordinary dream about her own death. It seems that all her life she had had this sort of dream on the eve of any misfortune. On the last occasion, when she woke in the morning, she said to her husband, "I am sure something dreadful is going to happen to me, for I have had a dream of the black bull pursuing me, but last night it overtook me and trampled me down under its feet". She died the following night after a sudden attack of inflammation.

About the year 1839, when Louisa Danson resided with her Uncle and Aunt, Colonel and Mrs. Tuite, in a large house in Boulogne, rue St. Martin, she was sitting up one night alone in the drawing room, and the old people were both ill. She had sent all the servants to bed and sat up to give the old folks their medicine at the appointed times. She was a very strong-minded person, not in the least degree nervous or fanciful. On this occasion she was reading a novel to pass the time. The room door was open, and all at once something attracted her notice. She looked up and saw the figure of a person standing at the door. She immediately got up, went towards the door. The figure retreated. She followed through the hall, then through the billiard room till it came to a door at the foot of the back stairs and there it vanished. She tried to open the door but it was locked on the other side. She then felt very queer, and perplexed. She retraced her steps, but to get at the part of the house where her Uncle and Aunt were, she had to pass the courtyard which was covered in, and the entrances locked. She looked through all the rooms and found everyone safe in bed. The following explanation was found for this curious circumstance. The house had formerly belonged to one of Napoleon's Officers who suddenly disappeared. No one ever knew what became of him. About the year 1840, the Tuite family returned to England, and no one ever lived in the house afterwards. It was ultimately pulled down, and the skeleton of a man was found in one of the cellars and was supposed to clear up the mystery of the disappearance of its former owner, who was discovered to have been murdered.

There was at Boulogne a family of the name of Callaghan whom we knew very well. Mr. Callaghan had been married three times, but at that time he had only one child, a daughter by the last wife. In his youth he went to Gibraltar as a wine merchant. He made a large fortune, married, and had a numerous family. On returning to his native land the ship was wrecked and all his family perished, likewise his fortune. The unfortunate man returned, recommenced life, made another fortune, had another wife and family, and again started for home, when again he was shipwrecked, and lost his wife, family and fortune. He, undaunted, returned a third time, and again married and made a fortune and succeeded at last in reaching England safely with his third wife and one daughter. The latter grew up a beautiful girl, the idol of her parents. At the age of 18 she fell into a deep decline. Everything was done to save her, but after consulting all the leading Physicians, her cure was declared hopeless, and a journey to a warm country was advised. They came to Boulogne *en route* for some more southern country, but she became so ill that they could go no further. At this time the miracles worked by Prince Hohenlohe* were much talked about and the family resolved to pray to him for a cure. A novena was begun in which all the friends joined. On the 9th day the invalid was taken to Church. At the communion she was carried to the Altar rails, and the instant she received Holy Communion was entirely cured and walked back to her seat without help. She lived for many years after, but was sometimes very delicate.

There were some Nuns at Boulogne called Les "Soeurs grises" who took in plain work and knitting. Mrs. Callaghan wanted some stockings knitted for her husband, so one day she called with him, giving the necessary directions. He was an Irishman of the biggest type, stout in proportion to his height. In due time the stockings were finished, but double the amount charged for than had been agreed upon. Mrs. Callaghan asked the reason why, and the Nun replied "Well madame, when Monsieur called with you, we saw him and he looked so enormous, we thought it impossible for the pattern to fit him so we made the stockings extra large. In fact, they were exactly one yard long, and wide in proportion".

One of our many friends was Mlle Chanlère; she used to lodge at the Ursuline Convent, her only sister being a Nun there. Their Father had been a gentleman of some consequence before the revolution, and judging from their large house must have had a

---

* Prince Hohenlohe - Alexander Leopold Franz Emmerich - Bishop of Sardica (1794-1849). He entered the Society of the Heart of Jesus in 1815. He settled in Bavaria in 1817 and soon after commenced praying for the cure of the sick. He is said to have had successes in Vienna. In 1821 the Pope refused to sanction this healing activity. Clementina Cox, Helen's sister, the Visitation nun, ascribed her miraculous cure, at the beginning of her religious life, to his prayers.

considerable fortune. Mlle was a remarkable person, and, to my mind, more agreeable, just the reverse of what we term "une dévote", a detestable class of people! Although she was a lady by birth, she sacrificed everything for religion, even dressing in the costume of a servant, and wearing a cap, as was the custom for the middle class of people in France. She occupied only one room at the top of the Convent, devoting her whole time and fortune to the poor. She rose very early everyday, went to Mass at 6 o'clock, spent an hour in the Church and made frequent visits to the Blessed Sacrament. The rest of the time was spent in visiting the prisoners, the poor, and doing other works of mercy. Very often she used to bring home the linen of the prisoners, and mend it with her own hands. She used to dine in the Convent refectory with pupils, and I well remember if any dainty child objected to eat an underdone piece of meat, fat or anything objectionable, the good creature would take it on her plate, and eat it, to prevent the girls from getting scolded. She worked a great deal for the Church, making and repairing Altar linen and vestments, for which she begged materials. It was Mlle Chanlère who first called to tell my family of the then new intitution of the "Propagation of the Faith", and to beg them to insert their names as subscribers, which they gladly did, and have ever since continued to support it. It was she also who informed my grandmother of an interesting prisoner confined in the gaol for not having a passport, but a very respectable young man. Being a stranger in Boulogne, and having no friends, my grandparents took him into their service, much to the horror of some of our English friends. I heard one lady exclaim, "Why, Mrs. Cox he might cut all your throats some night". The man was named Emile and turned out very well. He was the same that went in search of a Priest for Elizabeth when she was dying in London.

After dear Elizabeth's death, which I have already related, my grandparents took a house in Haunton Street, Kensington. It was a grand, comfortable house, and had the advantage of being near the Catholic Chapel. Mr. L'Abbé le Houx was the Priest, a very cross old gentleman, whom my sister Alicia called very bitterly the Abbé Prickles. "Houx" meaning holly. He very often dined with us, and as often made himself disagreeable by his remarks. On one occasion when coffee was served, he looked at his cup, stirred it with his spoon, and said to my sister, "Mademoiselle, le café, pour être bon, doit avoir trois qualités; il doit être chaud, il doit être fort,

*Dominic Le Houx

il doit être claire; ce cafe n'a pas ces qualités, il ne vaut rien, ce café là", all the while turning it with his spoon with real French vehemence. There was a young lady in the congregation in whom he took a great interest, as she was going to be a Nun. She went to take leave of some friends, and at the house of one of them, she met a gentleman who proposed to her, and she accepted. When the Abbé heard of her change of intention, he was very angry, and exclaimed, "If she will not be Nun, my John shall be a monk", meaning her brother. But John also got married to a Miss Roskell of Liverpool, and his sister became Mrs. Lynch. Their name was Kendal.

★ ★ ★

In the month of May of this year, my grandparents determined to return to their residence in Herefordshire, so my grandmother and sister went to prepare the house, which had to be entirely refurnished. I remained with the old people, my grandfather and his sister, almost blind. In due time we were sent for, and travelled to Hereford in a Post-Chaise and pair, and I shall never forget my feeling on that day. The elders were afraid of fresh air, and all the windows were kept closely shut, I being squeezed between the two old folks for a journey of 30 miles. I shall never forget the discomfort of those hours. At Hereford my grandfather's carriage met us at the Green Dragon Hotel and took us to Eaton Bishop. I was much delighted at the thought of seeing with my own eyes a place I had heard so much of, and I watched with great eagerness from the carriage window for the first sight of the village. When we drew up in front of the house, I was surprised to find it so large, but upon entering, found the rooms very small. My grandfather, who had had it rebuilt, thought it would make a nice snug place for him to retire to in his old age, and, with that intent, the sitting-rooms were all on a small scale, which to his idea constituted comfort, but he did not anticipate retiring with a family of grandchildren. It was nevertheless a dear, rambling old place and called "Green Court". I don't recollect how long all the repairs took, but when all was completed, the foreman asked my grandfather if he would like to mount the scaffolding before it was taken down, to see the magnificient view of the Black Mountains of Wales and the surrounding country. He consented to do so, and at the same time the workmen assembled to take a last look, when, lo and behold! The whole structure came down with a crash. In the hurry of the moment, my grandather slipped his arm down one of the chimneys, and so saved himself from an instant death, but in the fall one of the men seized his foot, so that both were suspended from the same chimney which, being quite new, gave way and they both fell to the ground. My grandfather broke his leg, and was lame ever after. The same leg was broken twice, once when he was 83 and again when he was 93.

In the reign of King Charles, "Green Court" had been the property of one of my ancestors, Richard Snead, for some time High Sheriff of Herefordshire. He married a daughter of the King's physician, Dr. Napier,* brother to the celebrated Napier, "The wizard of Oxford". Some years after, Green Court was rented by Mr. Dolman, and my dear husband was born there. On the day of his birth an extraordinary event occurred. Although he was the 6th child of his parents, he was the eldest son, therefore there were great rejoicings at his birth. The ringers were assembled to ring a "joy peal" on the then celebrated peal of fine bells, presented by Mrs. Witherstone. On that day my grandfather's woodmen were felling timber. One of the men, Tom Baker, was a bad man. His companions accused him of some disreputable conduct, which he denied. The others persisted that he was guilty. At last Baker exclaimed with an oath "If I did that, may God strike me dead". And at that moment the tree fell, and although all the men were out of reach, it actually bounded several times forward, and just touched the unhappy creature with its top twigs, but killed him on the spot. The consternation of the other men was great. The poor wife was working at Green Court and was informed of the event. The joy bells were changed to tolling, which superstitious people said was a bad omen to the new baby. Widow Baker lived to a great age and was a pensioner of the family till her death.

There is a stile at Green Court which is shown as the spot where an unfortunate Roundhead became headless during the civil wars. The family at Green Court were royalists, and the individual in question had wandered as far as Green Court as a spy; he was

---

* Napier - Sir Richard Napier (1605-1676) is perhaps the physician. He graduated M.D. in 1642 from Exeter College, Oxford. He was nephew and heir of Richard Napier (not his brother) who was celebrated as a clergyman and astrologer who seemed to possess miraculous powers. He was no doctor but practised Phisick. He, too, was a graduate of Exeter College. Presumably he is the "Wizard of Oxford".

recognized at once by one of the villagers in his true character. A struggle ensued. The spy was overcome, and the other having a bill hook in his hand cut off his head. He was one of the Scotch army, men stationed in Hereford under David Lesley.

It was at Green Court that we first became acquainted with the young Dolmans, and my sisters were sent to Hartpury Convent.* My sister Alicia was very given to many childish escapades which were long remembered in the family. One day there was a dinner party, and Alicia was to go down to dessert, and was properly dressed for the occasion. While she was waiting for the summons to the dining room, she went into my grandfather's room to survey herself in the long glass. She thought she could improve her appearance by a few changes, so she began by cutting her hair short; she then got some soap and plastered it on her head until she made her hair shine which she brushed close down to her head; then she procured a long darning needle and two glass beads; she made holes through her ears with the needle, and tied a bead in each with coarse worsted, and in that guise went down to the company, thinking herself quite a lady of fashion. The reception is better imagined than described. She was original in her ideas all her life, and grew up very talented, as well as amiable and good. She became a Benedictine Nun and died at St. Benedict's Priory, 1862.

Some of the rooms of Green Court had strange stories connected with them. That inhabited by an ancestor, Mr. Snead, attracted my attention. His story was a sad one. He was the eldest of that branch of the family, and inherited the paternal property. Being wild and reckless, he spent his all, and was thrown destitute on the world. His brother Richard had risen in the world as his spendthrift brother went down, being quite of a different character. He was very kind and affectionate by nature, and gave the unfortunate scapegrace the run of his house, which he accepted, and made it his home for the rest of his life. One morning he did not make his appearance at breakfast. A servant was sent to his room to ask if he was ill. He said "No", but that he did not intend to go down any more, as he was going to die that day. He remained in the same state, not complaining of any illness until sunset, when he actually did die.

In another room a Mrs. Hunt died. She had been born in the same room 130 years before. After she became a widow, she went

---

* Hartpury, Gloucestershire. French refugee nuns settled here and built a Chapel in 1830.

to reside with a married daughter, who, 50 years after, died of old age, after which the old lady returned to her natal home, and after another long visit, departed this life.

Many things interested me in the grounds of Green Court. Among others, there was a summer house which then stood on a hillock, but had been transfered from another place on rollers. Those who disapproved the manoeuvre christened it "Sam's Folly", as the owner who had had it done at some expense was named Samuel. There was also a stone table on which was carved the names of many generations, most of them quite illegible. A very large dovecot, capable of holding many hundred pairs of pigeons, was the object of some curiosity. It was put up at the time the house was built long before. The law was made to prohibit the building of such places, or to re-erect those which had gone to decay, so consequently my grandfather was very careful to keep this one in good repair. There was also a large pond, well supplied with fish, called "Bullocks" pool. In an adjoining field there were the ruins of an old cottage which fell to decay after the suicide of the last tenant, who hanged himself. I used to look at the ruin with great awe, meditating on the awful end of the unhappy man, and tracing out the marks of the old garden, then overgrown with brambles. The barn was still made use of by the occupier of the Court lands.

One fine day of the summer of 1830, I, with a party of friends returning from a walk, took shelter in the barn from the heat of the sun. After a time we heard a loud bellow and, to our dismay, a huge bull was standing in the doorway confronting us; there was no escape so we determined to make a grand rush at the beast, which, happily for us, scampered off, leaving us free to gain the stile.

The family attended Mass on Sundays at Hereford, quite an undertaking. I was always one of the party who went in the Phaeton; my sister Alicia generally rode, and my Aunt had her own pony-carriage. One day, the 15th of August, we were overtaken by a fearful thunderstorm. When we got about half way home, it became so alarming that we sought shelter at a farm house, where we put up the carriage. We had only been there a few minutes when a tremendous crash came which sent us all down upon our knees in an instant, for everyone thought their last hour had come. The thunderbolt had fallen close to the door of the house, splitting a very large tree from top to bottom. Just before we took shelter, we met a man on horseback. The animal had taken fright and was galloping at a terrific rate. The poor rider looked the image of despair. They were both struck dead just after. The storm lasted all day. We arrived home late in the evening, very grateful for our escape.

We had a chapel in the house where we frequently had mass, for constantly Priests were staying with us, sometimes for months together. As a rule, "the good gentlemen" (the term then applied by old Catholics to Priests) from Hereford came over at all the indulgences[1] to hear confessions and say Mass. Once a month, or eight times a year, was the most that even the most fervent Catholics ever thought of going to Holy Communion; indeed it was considered rather profane for a lay person to receive oftener; nor did Priests encourage the practice. A much more elaborate preparation was required, and always a three days' retirement and meditation was advised, and followed, by those who were in earnest. This idea probably arose from the difficulty of receiving the Sacrament during the times of persecution, and then from the fewness of Priests. Frequent Communion only became general after the establishment of the Hierarchy in England. Some people went so far as to refuse Holy Communion on their death-bed, thinking, in full faith, that they were not worthy.

How differently those things were managed then to what they are now! People then had such a dread of what ought to be their greatest comfort in life. Several days were always given to the preparation, and on the day of confession, everyone seemed to have a load on their mind, no one speaking. It was our custom to send the carriage to fetch his "Reverence", and how we young people used to look out of the window, waiting for its return and if, by chance it returned empty, it was quite a relief to get a reprieve for a time. When the Priest did come, his entertainment was somewhat stiff and restrained. We all met at dinner, and, at the usual time afer dessert, the ladies left the dining room. Soon after that the gentlemen followed, not to the drawing room, but each one to his own apartment. In due time his "reverence" went into the Chapel, and then the confessions began. There was no general meeting again that night, but everyone remained at their own devotions. For my part I used to read Baker's[2] meditations, and I believe

---

1 "indulgences" - holy days on which a special indulgence could be gained.

2 Baker, David - known usually by his name in religion - Augustine. O.S.B. (1575-1641) Spiritual director of English Benedictine nuns at Cambrai.

others did the same until it was time for night prayers, which were said in public, after which all retired to rest. The following day the scene was quite changed. Everyone was bright, happy and cheer-ful.

*   *   *

The routine of our daily life was very regular. We rose very early, heard Mass, said our morning prayers in common, and then my sister and I spent an hour in practising music or drawing. In the summer we two rode out on horse-back, with old Davis to accom-pany us. Breakfast was at 8 o'clock. My grandfather generally walked for 2 hours beforehand. After breakfast the family sepa-rated for their respective employments. My grandmother to her house-keeping, my Aunt to her own room, where she spent the time in praying and doing embroidery the whole day, except when she joined the family at meals, until 8 in the evening, when she came down to play a rubber of whist, after which a meditation from Challoner was read, followed by night prayers, always recited by my grandfather, unless a Priest was present. He often exclaimed during the examination of conscience, "O my God, have mercy on me, a most miserable sinner". It seemed to come from his very heart, as if he were thinking aloud. We young people used to laugh, seeing the regular edifying life he used to lead, so charitable, gen-tle, and kind. He never said a cross word to anyone or did anything contrary to the Christian gentleman. He generally spent his morn-ings reading or writing, then retired to his room to pray, and to make his toilet. My sister and self generally spent the morning in the library, studying. Dinner was at 3 o'clock; after that we walked or drove. Tea was at six. My grandfather always took a walk after tea. If it were a wet day, he used an empty room for that purpose. During that time the ladies generally played music, or read some book of devotion at that hour. When the card hour arrived we all played in turn, that is, the juniors relieved each other in amusing the seniors. Indeed, it was no amusement to us. I never liked whist since I had such a dose of it then. My grandfather was punctuality exemplified. He generally had his watch by his side, allowing him-self one hour for dinner, and half-an-hour for breakfast and tea. He never took lunch or supper, but had a glass of spirits before going to bed. About this time my grandmother died, and for the 9 years that grandfather survived her, he lived alone. He had another house in Hereford, where he occasionally lived with his sister, his wife having died there. His illness was very short; he had a bad cold and kept to his bed a few days. Being delirious he insisted upon going into another room, where he said his wife was waiting for him. His wish was gratified, and he was quite contented, appearing to see his wife at the foot of the bed, and said "Yes, my dear, I am coming"! He partially recovered from that attack, and even had the family assembled for night prayers in his room. He made the sign of the Cross and said a fervent "Amen" at the end. When the servant went up to the bed to see if he was comfortable for the night, he found him already dead. He expired immediately at the conclusion of the prayers. He had been to Communion a short time before, and it was remarked that he was so wonderfully devout on the occasion. All were much struck. He died on the 21st January, 1840. He was born 1746, and he remembered having seen the heads of the Scotch Lords who were beheaded for their participation in the rebellion of 1745. When he was quite a small boy he caught up the popular rhyme of the 5th of November as follows:-

"Remember, remember the 5th of November,
Gunpowder treason and plot,
For I see no reason why gunpowder treason
Should ever be forgot."

Then followed some verses about the burning of the Pope, and the child thought himself very clever to be able to learn this fine composition, being quite innocent of its purport; so he went very early on the 5th of November, to his Aunt's bedroom and sang it with all his might as a serenade. She opened the door and said very kindly "Come in Sammy. I will teach you how to remember that song", and she gave him a sound whipping which, in truth, he found no reason should ever be forgot. He was educated at the Bar and had chambers at Lincon's Inn, but Mrs. Witherstone, his Aunt and the owner of "Green Court", having lost her only son, proposed in the first place to adopt my great Aunt, but on condition that she should be brought up a protestant, she herself being such; but my great grandfather's reply was such as proved him to be a true Christian; he thanked his cousin for her kind offer, but he added "Much as I value your proposal, I value my daughter's soul much more, and must decline". Mrs. Witherstone then made the offer to my grandfather without the conditon of changing his religion, but that he should give up his profession and reside at Green Court, which he agreed to do. He must have had a dull life for a young man; his relative was a person of strong will and primitive habits. She rose at 4 o'clock every morning, and generally took a ride on horseback before her 6 o'clock breakfast, and expected my grandfather to accompany her. After her first meal she made the round of the village to see that the women were all at their spinning wheels, or other work, reprimanding severely all idlers. On the other hand, she was a mother to all, giving or lending money as the case might be; in fact, she managed the whole village and was held in great respect as well as awe. In her own household she enforced the observance of strict rules. Everyone had to be in bed at 8 o'clock.

On one occasion, someone called at the house after that hour, to the great consternation of the inmates, who observed that no person of good intent could come to disturb the house at that unreasonable hour of the night. The good old lady reigned without control till she was some years past 90, and died regretted by all. My grandfather was expected to conform to all the habits of his Aunt. He found it very irksome to retire for the night at 8 o'clock in the summer. Therefore, one beautiful evening, he was reading in bed, which he did constantly, it being broad daylight, when he was discovered, and his Aunt reprimanded him severely, and told him that if he ever did the like again, she would disinherit him.

Another time he had an illness during which she nursed him with extreme care and as soon as he became convalescent, it was decided that change of air would do him good, so it was decided that he should go to Abergavenny for a time. He was much delighted at the idea of freedom without the risk of displeasing his Aunt. She had insisted upon his wearing his nightcap all day since his illness, for fear of his taking cold and he was to travel in it under his hat. However, he resolved to get rid of the obnoxious appendage as soon as he was out of sight. In this he was disappointed for, just on the point of starting, she called the servant and said, "John, you must watch my nephew, and if he takes off his nightcap on the journey, you must let me know". Of course, the servant was obliged to obey, or give up a good place. My grandfather wisely came to the conclusion that it was better to comply with such distasteful commands than to forfeit a nice estate and return to plead at the Bar. One of his favourite amusements was writing poetry. The following was written on an old woman named Margaret Scott.

Stop passenger, until my life you read.
The living may get knowledge from the dead.
Five times five years I led a virgin life;
Ten times five years I was a virtuous wife;
Ten times five years I lived a widow chaste.
Now, tired of this mortal life, I rest.
Between my cradle and my grave hath been
Eight mighty Kings of Scotland and a Queen.
Four times five years a common wealth I saw.
Ten times the subject rose against the law.
Twice did I see old Prelacy put down,
And twice the cloak was humbled by the gown.
An end of Stewart's race I saw - nay more,
I saw my country sold for English or.
Such desolation in my time hath been,
I have an end of all perfection seen.

At Green Court there was a "hiding hole"viz, a place of conceatment for Priests in times of persecution. This one was at the side of a stack of chimnies; the entrance to it was at the top of a cupboard in the dining room at the right-hand side of the fire place. A sliding panel was removed for anyone who wished to avail himself of it. In the time of Mrs. Witherstone, an uncle of that lady claimed her hospitality: Edmund Cox,* a monk of the Benedictine order from the monastery of St. Omer's in France. I do not know in what year he came over, but he paid a visit to his cousin. She, although a protestant, secreted him for a considerable period in the "hiding hole", taking him food at night. At last he went away to return to his monastery, promising to write to her when he got back, but she never received a letter. Whether he was discovered to be a Catholic Priest, and made away with, she never heard, so she often bewailed his supposed fate, saying that he never would have forgotten her kindness, had he escaped.

* Edmund Cox died 1748

The Chapel at Hereford at this time was very small and in a very obscure part of the town.* It had a congregation of about 100 people among the real poor. There were many who had been wealthy yeomen a few years back, but had been ruined by the heavy fines exacted from Catholics. The mission passed from Jesuit hands to Benedictines about this time. Who the original founder was I never heard, but my grandfather remembered a Lord Cahir, commonly called Mr. Butler, as a Priest, and a Mr. Horn. Curious stories used to be told of these gentlemen, and in those times many quaint occurrences used to take place when a priest tried to carry out the Ceremonies of Palm Sunday. Calling to his old factotem he said, "Molly, my boy", (her name was Mary), and after blessing the palms, he turned round to her, "Molly, my boy, distribute the palms to the company". He generally had a sand-glass before him when he preached, and, if he felt inclined to prolong his sermon, he would say "Well my lads, what say you to another glass?" and if no objection was raised, he would turn the glass for another spell! Most likely, these eccentricities were resorted to, in order to deprive the ceremonies of a religious character, to the uninitiated, at a time when informers crept in everywhere, long before the repeal of the penal laws against Catholics. My grandfather had to submit to the greatest indignities occasionally before the Emancipation Act was passed in 1829, as did other gentlemen. If they were seen to ride a good horse, any common fellow who chose could offer him five pounds for it, and it might be a very valuable animal, and the rider had no option but to give it up, or to be informed against for not paying double taxes and other liabilities, which were not strictly enforced, but which could be brought under the notice of a magistrate. My grandfather was also much annoyed by depredators in his woods, who used to cut down young trees for firewood, and then offer the ashes for sale at the House for washing. If any remarks were made, the answer would be "Well Squire, you don't pay double taxes; I'll inform against you". I remember one very obnoxious old man named Landman, a great persecutor in the above line, and a poacher. He was a regular recipient of charity from us. In my time, he was very old and looked very venerable with his long white hair. He perished with his name. He had an only daughter whom I visited during a very long illness, after which she died.

* Hereford's first public Chapel was built by Fr. William Horne in 1790 and licensed in 1791. A succession of Jesuits served the chapel up to 1857 when they were followed by Benedictines.

Among our neighbours at Eaton Bishop was a Lady Southampton and her family, 2 sons and one daughter. She was the founder of a sect then called Evangelical. She held meetings in her own
house, at which she preached and prayed. She was extremely
charitable, giving away food and clothing to all the villagers who
chose to attend her Chapel. She generally wore a queer bonnet like
a long tunnel, made of black silk, and paid her visits from house to
house in a pony carriage, making one of her sons hold the beast
until she came out. That sort of life so disgusted the young man,
that, as soon as he became his own master, he set no bounds to his
folly, as a natural reaction to so much restraint. One day Lady
Southampton called upon the wife of a neighbouring Squire and
began to lecture her on her worldly life. The lady retorted by saying
that she went to Church every Sunday and considered that quite
sufficient for salvation. Her ladyship then remarked, "There is but
one real Christian in the village, and that is Mrs. Cox, although she
is a Catholic".

In the winter of 1829, Mr. Brigham*, brother of the Priest in
Hereford, paid us a visit of some days. He was a very fascinating
man of about 40 and a widower, and was much struck by my sister
Alicia, and consequently they fell in love. After a time it was an
understood thing that a marriage should take place. The following
September was to be the great triennial music meeting. Mr.
Brigham was invited and I was to make my Début at the Balls and
concerts, which were to take place on three succeeding days. Very
great was our delight at the anticipation of what was to be. All the
new dresses, concert dresses and bonnets and finery of every kind
were sent home. I really think that I thought of nothing else for
weeks and months before the time. The first day of the festival was
to be a Tuesday, and whether from excitement or what I know not,
but Alicia looked very unwell. On the Sunday she was too unwell
to drive to Mass, so she remained at home. When we arrived home,
I ran upstairs to our bedroom to find Alicia, and exclaimed, "Oh,
Lishy I have seen William Brigham, and he is coming to dine". My
sister made no reply, but in a few minutes fell back in her chair saying, "Oh! I am so ill". She looked deadly pale, and had a violent
hemorrhage - she had ruptured a blood vessel! As soon as possible,
I gave the alarm. Everyone rushed to the room in consternation.
The doctor was sent for, and pronounced the case hopeless, as
nothing could stop the hemorrhage which continued until the

* Mr. Brigham was the brother of Fr. J. H. Brigham S. J. (1823-1825)

patient seemed to have no blood left. By the time the Brighams arrived, she was quite insensible, and apparently dying. The Priest returned at once to Hereford for the holy oils, and it was very late before he got back. He gave her the last anointing; all her senses were gone. She could neither see or hear. The Priest absolutely shouted the 'Salve Regina' in her ear to try and rouse her but without effect. The next day she seemed to fall into her agony, and became possessed with wonderful strength, so that it took two women to prevent her from leaping out over the head of the bed. After that, she relapsed into a sort of trance, and she was kept alive by having liquids poured into her mouth, drop by drop. She was so near death that all the preparations for laying her out were made. This lasted for several days, and one morning when I returned to the sick room after breakfast, I found the door locked. Thinking that all was over, and fearing to be told the truth, I locked myself into the Library and was not missed for several hours. At last someone came, but I would not let them in for fear they should tell what I so much dreaded to hear. At last I was made to understand that my darling sister was still alive, aand I was induced to go to her room. Thus many weary days and hours passed on, and still she remained in the same state. On the eventful Tuesday night to which I had looked forward for so long, it was rumoured in the Ball-room that "Miss Cox was dead", which created a great impression, and cast a gloom over all who knew her. On the following Sunday, a week from the first attack, my sister was still like a corpse and could scarcely be perceived to breathe. What prompted me, I know not, but I applied a bottle of strong ammonia to her nose; the effect was instantaneous. She opened her eyes, then yawned and stretched out her arms and legs, and immediately swallowed some chicken broth. After a time she spoke, and asked where she had been. From then she began to recover.

For my part, I concluded that this dreadful event had occurred to punish me for my worldliness and I made a vow was that if my dear sister recovered, I would renounce all balls and plays for the future. This vow afterwards cancelled by the Bishop, at the request of my parents, who became cognisant of it when I scrupled to attend a Ball they wished me to go to. Mr. Brigham was my director, and I asked him to tell my parents. Of course, there was a row, and they allowed me to stay away. Although I attended a few afterwards, I never went to any public amusement of my own accord, and in later years, when my husband knew of this, he never asked me.

In the year 1828, when we left Boulogne, the house was let for two years, and after that time, it was necessary to return to settle affairs; accordingly my grandmother decided to go herself and take me with her. We started on our journey, and when we reached Dover, we heard a report that a revolution had broken out in France. Many of the passengers refused to proceed, but my grandmother, being a resolute person, determined to go. Accordingly we landed at Boulogne and went straight to our house, which was not far from the prison. I shall never forget the horrors of that time. We were kept awake the whole night by the tumultuous noise of the prisoners who were evidently vociferating, cursing, swearing and using the most awful language, trying at the same time to force open the doors; the battering on which made a most hollow sound which re-echoed through the dead of the night. The next day we went to our friends in the Lower town. We lived in the Upper town, which was that part round the old Castle, and was within the walls of the City, and strong ramparts and gates, which were locked and guarded every night. About 10 o'clock that night we set off to walk home, my grandmother, George and myself. When we reached la grande rue, which was on our way home, we found such a dense crowd of rabble all crying out: "A bas Charles dix, vive la République", that we could with difficulty push through. At last we got up to the hill to within sight of our gate, through which we were obliged to pass; but it was actually besieged and a great battle was going on between the Royalists defending the King's arms, and the republicans, trying to pull them down; at last the latter prevailed and got their ladders up to the walls, scaled them and tore down the object of their rage. In the midst of the conflict, my brother, who was a great royalist, felt so provoked that he shouted out, "Vive Charles dix"; in an instant the infuriated mob rushed upon us, when my grandmother, with admirable coolness, exclaimed in her polite tone, "Messieurs, je vous en prie, faites places aux Dames"; immediately the ruffians made way for us, and escorted us safe through the place and we got home.

We remained a month at Boulogne this time, during which time we saw much of our old friends. Among others was a Mr. & Mrs. Muller, two sons and two daughters. Mrs. Muller had been a school fellow of my grandmother at the Ursuline Convent at

Boulogne, before the revolution of 1794, and became a novice in the same Convent, which was seized during the reign of Terror, and the Nuns put to death. Among the community in prison was the novice Miss Byham from the West Indies, and of the citizens there was a Mr. Muller, a merchant. All there, Priests, Nuns, Laymen and Laywomen, high and low, all were huddled together. Mr. Muller took compassion on Miss Byham and offered himself to be her protector for life. Her friends advised her under the circumstances to accept the offer, and the marriage ceremony was performed by a Priest. As they all sat at table during dinner, they joined hands under the table, and so became man and wife. The family were all very holy. The eldest girl, who was very beautiful, became a Nun of the Visitation, and died Superior at Boulogne. After our return to England in the month of July 1832, the Brighams came to see us. We all rode out together on horseback and in returning, whilst passing through a lane, Alicia's horse shied, and threw her over its head. She fell on the hard road upon her head and felt for a moment as if her neck was broken. It was the feast of Mount Carmel, and she attributed her preservation to Our Blessed Lady, whom she invoked. She got up uninjured, which was considered miraculous, and remounted her horse, feeling none the worse for her adventure.

Soon after this incident, my father, mother and the rest of the family arrived from France after an absence of 15 years, to take up their abode in England. We went to meet them at Hereford and they all looked fearfully tired and ill from the journey. The heat of the weather and confinement in the coaches was a great trial. They had come from Le Mans through Normandy. Cholera was then raging, and my dear mother took it, and nearly died on the road. They were detained at Seize* on that account. Afterwards my sister Euphemia caught the same malady, and in crossing the Bristol Channel, had to be placed quite close to the funnel of the steamer to infuse warmth into her. Her face was quite blue and everyone on board kept away for fear of infection. At the Hotel I had the greatest difficulty in distinguishing her from my other sister, Sarah. They looked so much alike, but when I got to know them, they were very different from each other. Poor Euphemia was, of course, very weak, and when we got back home, she took my arm and I led her into her room. I looked at her in wonder for I thought

* Sées

I had never seen anything so beautiful. Her features were Grecian in form, her eyes were large, beautiful and dark blue. Her skin as white and smooth as the purest marble. All her movements were so graceful that it was many weeks before I could look at her without being struck by her demeanour; her expressions and conversation were equally prepossessing. Everyone was fascinated by her, so that when she went into company, a group at once gathered around her to hear and see her. She was a universal favourite. Sarah was also very attractive, but she was quite a child, and more reserved than her sister. They were both proficient in music, drawing, and what we called "accomplishments".

Mary Anne, a younger sister, did not strike me at all as being beautiful, but she was taller than the other two and very elegant in figure. She was very clever as an historian and antiquarian, very proficient in learning languages, and in music and drawing. Richard was a fat, good-natured boy of 11 years old, very mischievous, but of a loving disposition. We all spent the summer of 1832, together at Green Court, and then we parted once again. The seniors, that is my grandparents, wanted to spend the winter at Cheltenham, and Alicia and myself went to take care of them. My parents and the younger family remained at Eaton.

Mrs. J. T. Dolman, Née Anne Helen Cox who died 1891 with her husband, who died 1867 and one of her sons. They lived in her brother's house Souldern, Oxon.

The Second Period
of my Life, 1833

It was in the early spring of the year 1833 that I first saw my future husband. My sister and self were spending this summer with our grandparents at Cheltenham. John Dolman had come up on business about his sister's marriage, and hearing that a family of the name of Cox was living in Cheltenham, he immediately called to enquire if we were the same people he knew in Herefordshire. Although the family knew the Dolmans, as they lived in my grand-father's house at Eaton, still I had never met them and knew them only by name. On this memorable day, we were sitting in the draw-ing room in the afternoon, when a servant came in and said that a gentleman was downstairs and wished to see my grandmother. He had not been shown up because she was unwell, and it was doubtful if she could see anyone. A name was given by the servant which no one could make out. After guessing for sometime, I, in a sort of inspiration said "Oh, it must be John Dolman". My grandmother repeated my words and said "What nonsense! what makes you think that. What would bring any of them to Cheltenham"! It certainly was strange, as I did not know them. My grandmother went downstairs and came back laughing and said "Well Helen, you are right. It is one of the Dolmans, John the eldest son, and my godson, and he is coming back to dinner". He came and we thought him an interesting young man, very shy, extremely fair, with a lot of light curly hair. He was in his 22nd year. After he had gone away, of course we girls began to make remarks about him, and Alicia remarked that he would make a good beau for me. I felt very indignant, and replied "Indeed I don't want him. He is much too young for me". The next day he came again and accompanied us to a party. In a day or two he went away, and I thought no more about him. My sister's comb fell off at the party, and he kept a piece of it, thinking it was mine, I only found it among his treasures after his death.

The history of John Dolman's early life has always struck me as particulary sad. Much younger than his sisters, he became their protector whilst a mere boy, and they looked up to him for advice.

He lost his mother when he was only 6 years old. She died in her 34th year, having had ten children. The poor things soon had another mother, who was very unkind to them. When John was still young, his father took him to college where he remained until his education was finished. His maternal grandfather had adopted all his daughter's children, and it was to his home that John went upon leaving school. Mr. Griffiths was a great bigot, though a good-hearted man, and wanted to make his grandchildren turn Protestant, but they had all been too well grounded in their faith to change. Poor John went through a kind of martyrdom for his religion, and on Fridays kept out of the house, to escape the persecution for not eating meat. One day, when he came in from fishing, his grandfather was in an unusual good humour and said very kindly (which surprised his grandson). "John I have ordered some dinner to be kept for you. Go and eat it". Of course John felt very grateful, and wondered at the change come over the old man. When he had finished his meal his grandfather said, "Well John, do you feel the worse for your dinner"? "No", said John, "Much better". Then said the old gentleman, "I tell you, you have been eating meat"! These young people used to club their pocket money together to hire a conveyance to go to Mass on Sundays. The old gentleman, although so bigoted, behaved very well in the main, for he left all his fortune to them, making each one independent. It was then that John began to study medicine. He was the first eldest son of his family that had been obliged to take to a profession for 500 years. At this time it was only younger sons who sought a profession.

A curious story is told of John's father, Robert Dolman, who resided at Liège in Germany, and died there 1792. He had married a 2nd wife, and, in consequence, the father and son were not on very good terms. After the son left Douai College, he went to reside with his maternal grandfather, whilst his father remained at Liège. The affairs of the family were in a very embarrassed state, and the father had obtained an act of Parliament to sell his estates, which were entailed. It appears that the father had something on his mind relating to family business, which he wanted to communicate to his son. One night he was taken suddenly ill, and expressed a desire to see his son, and he asked that he should be sent for. In the meantime, his son was at his own house in bed and asleep. Suddenly he woke up, having dreamt that his father was dying and wanted to see him. He fell asleep and dreamt the same thing again. He woke up and thought it a foolish dream and composed himself to sleep a third time. For the third time the dream was repeated. He was then convinced that there must be something very unnatural, so he got up, dressed himself, and set off for his father's house. When he got half way, he met one of his father's servants, who accosted him and told him that his father was very ill, and wanted to see him. He proceeded on his journey, but when he reached the house, his father had just expired, and he was told that his last words were to inquire if his son had come. It was never known what he wished to say, but it was probable that he wanted to advise his son not to let the sale of the estate go on.

His father sold the family estate when barely of age, being ill-advised by dishonest trustees, who are supposed to have made profit by it; and, being misled by false friends, he received a sum of money the very day he became of age, quite inadequate to the value of the estate. He afterwards filed a petition in Chancery to get it cancelled, but having received the money, nothing could be done. He was a reckless improvident man, and what he did not squander on himself he left to his 2nd wife and her children, not leaving a penny to the elder family. Thus, being left so independent, John developed a remarkable self-reliant, firm character, with a strong will and indomitable energy, so that he was looked up to and respected by all. He was a thorough Catholic, totally free from the least taint of human respect, at a time when Catholics were looked upon as beings of an inferior order. If he happened to be at a dinner party on a meagre day, and meat was offered to him, he would simply say, "No thank you, I do not eat meat today". He was a decided enemy to anything like falsehood, hypocrisy or deceit, and, though so inflexible and firm, was of a most affectionate disposition. He was not fond of general society or the gaieties of the world, but was deeply attached to those he loved, and was so generous and unselfish that he would have given his life for them. Such was the character of the slight, fair young man whom Providence had ordained to be my protector for thirty years of my life. I looked down upon him when I first knew him, because my beau ideal of a husband was a gay, fashionable officer of middle age, and a man of the world of society, who would enable me to enjoy myself in the gay world. Vain as I was, I had constantly prayed that, if it were God's will that I should lead a married life, he would give me a husband with whom I could serve him and save my soul. Sometime before I met John Dolman, I had especially prayed that I might soon meet with the person destined for me, and certainly my prayer was granted. John never placed any obstacle in my way by requiring me to lead a worldly life; he was an enemy to extravagance in dress or worldly show, and loved solitude and retirement with those he loved. I never had any difficulty with him in keeping my word to avoid useless amusements.

During our stay at Cheltenham, Alicia and I had many pleasant walks in the mornings. The gentlemen of the Berkeley Hunt were a great nuisance. They used to assemble round the Plough Hotel to criticise the ladies, so that no young lady could walk out in the afternoon unless they had a matron or gentlemen at their command, to serve as protector. As we had neither, we had to take our walk in the forenoon. I liked the gay shops of Cheltenham and the busy streets, and, being very vain, liked to be fashionably dressed and show off my pretty feet and ankles, which I was once told were the best in Cheltenham. Alicia liked the fields and retirement of the country, but notwithstanding our different tastes, we were bosum friends. My vanity was such that I am surprised I am still alive to write these lines in 1872.

In the following spring, we all returned to Eaton, and spent the summer at Green Court. In the Autumn, my grandparents, Alicia and I went to Worcester to winter there. Many of my grandfather's relations lived there, among others, Sir Thomas Winnington. His family were great friends of a Mrs. Thomas, and we met them at her house. A curious tradition is told of this house. Charles II took refuge in it, and the marks of the bullets are still to be seen. This was after the battle of Worcester. We often visited Mr. Hornyold at Blackmore Park, and on one occasion he presented us all with tickets for the hunt ball, which we amply enjoyed. We met the Reverend Mr. Tristram S. J.* at his house. The chapel at Worcester was considered the best modern one before the revival of Gothic Churches by Pugin Senior. It was built by the Jesuits at the cost of £2,000. The Priest at this time was Father Tristram, an exceedingly kind old man, who had formerly been at Liège before the Stonyhurst days. He was a hardworking zealous Priest, and visited each of his flock every day. Of course, he could not give much time to each, and seldom sat down. I fancy I can hear him now in his cheerful voice saying "Well, how are you all today", and such like greetings. One Sunday in 1833 we went to Mass; our seats were in the gallery. In the body of the Church, I saw a young man with very light hair, but could not see his face; an extraordinary sensation came over me at once, I know not why, and John Dolman passed through my mind. I certainly had not thought of him since the year before at Cheltenham. After Mass was over, we returned home, and soon after that, someone knocked at the door. The same queer feeling came over me, and who should be shown into the drawing room but John Dolman; he had come on purpose to see me; he remained a few days and when he left, he enclosed in a letter to my grandmother one for me, which was an offer of marriage, and which was to be given to me, if approved by my parents. It was delivered to me, and the affair was talked over. John went to Eaton to see my parents, and was accepted as my future husband. He then returned to York. My parents came to see us at Worcester, leaving the younger members of the family at home. We all left Worcester in the spring of 1834, and returned to Eaton together. We travelled with post-horses and

* Joseph Tristram at Worcester, 1837-1838

remained some hours at Little Malvern Court, and took luncheon with Mr. and Mrs. William Berington. We then continued our journey and arrived at Eaton that night. This summer passed quickly. John Dolman came to visit us. It was 3 days journey from York to Eaton, but he travelled night and day, and did it in 2 days and one night. Young men always preferred the outside of the coach to the interior, and indeed some ladies also, but it was not considered the thing for ladies to do; therefore we were never allowed to do it. On one occasion, after he had made up his mind to start on this journey, having reasons for telling no one, an old woman came to the house he was staying at, and wanted to tell his fortune. He refused and told her to go away, but she said "I can tell you something young gentleman. You are going to make a long journey to see the lady you are to be married to", he felt very much surprised, as he knew no one could have told her of his intentions.

Just at this time my aunt set fire to her room, and endangered the house. She had the habit of staying up very late at night, saying her long prayers, so that she never retired to rest until long after the others were asleep. All the rooms on the first floor were given up to the seniors when the family were all at Green Court, whilst the juniors used the rooms on the ground floor, I slept between the two, going from one to the other as circumstances might require. On the eventful night of the fire, the poor old lady was not well, so she intended to retire. That was at 10 o'clock. I took a little mixture to her just before, which she told me to put on the table. Then she wished me goodnight. She never would allow anyone, even at that time of her life, to attend upon her, and nothing offended her more than being watched. After I left her, I went to the opposite room to say goodnight to the old people. That was soon over, and on leaving their room, I heard a dreadful exclamation from my aunt: "Good God! What have I done". I looked in, and found the room in a blaze, the flames had already reached the ceiling and the bed was on fire. Of course, I gave the alarm, and those who were at supper downstairs came up, and all the servants were on the spot immediately. Poor Aunt, of course, was taken out at once, only half dressed. She presented a most pitiable spectacle and sat in the corner of the room where she was moved to, saying, "Oh dear! what have I done". Providence had so arranged that on the preceding day the housekeeper, who had been using the step ladder, a mop and bucket, should, to save herself the trouble of taking them down stairs, have put them in a cupboard outside my Aunt's door. These instruments were the means of extinguishing the fire. Two or three men attempted to drag down the bed hangings which were firmly fixed, and at last my father succeeded, and threw the blazing mass out of the window. The fire had already burnt the ceiling, and was making its way to the upper room; every scrap of furniture was burnt, and all the panes of glass in the window were broken. At last the fire was extinguished and poor aunt pacified. The room had only just been newly furnished, and the poor old soul was so pleased with it.

It was during this summer that my friend Amelia Gowland was married to her cousin Henry Horn. If she could only have foreseen the end! The parents only objected on the plea that he had no means. He was a barrister and, being a younger brother, had no private fortune excepting a fellowship at Magdalen College, which he had to resign at his marriage. The wedding was a gay one, and my sister Alicia was bridesmaid. They took up their residence in London and had a large family of sons and daughters. Being industrious, he was successful at the Bar, and was able, after a time, to take a large house and live in style. After Mr. Gowland's (senior) death, the grandfather went to live with Amelia, and at his death, she came in for a nice income, as he divided his property between Amelia and her sister. He was to be buried at Eaton Bishop and Mr. Horn accompanied the coffin from London to Cagebrook. The melancholy cortège arrived at night. The coffin was placed in the hall of his own house, and Mr. Horn retired to a room where supper had been prepared for him by an old servant who had charge of the house. She waited upon him and was concerned to find that he ate so little. He related to her the details of her master's last illness, and she in return told him all she had to say; among other domestic matters, that the cow was ill. She then wished him goodnight, and Mr. Horn retired to his room. The next day was Sunday. Mr. Horn came down at about 8 o'clock by the back stairs, to ask for some hot water to shave, as he said, to save Ann Taylor the trouble of going up, she having no one to help her, and he asked about the cow. Instead of returning the way he came down, he passed through the hall, opened a cupboard and took out a gun, which he took up to his room by the front stairs, so that Mrs. Taylor did not see him. Afterwards she remembered that she had heard a loud noise in his room, which she thought must be the fall of his washing stand and crockery; but as nothing followed, and no bell was rung, she took no further notice, and went up with them, and knocked at the door several times; receiving no answer, she became alarmed and told her husband. They got a ladder, and the husband set it against the window and went up to look in - what was his horror, when he saw poor Mr. Horn lying in pool of blood upon the floor with the gun by his side; he had placed the muzzle of the gun in his mouth; and so blown out his brains! He had been dead long enough before the body was removed, for the blood to congeal round his head and retain the outline of his profile, which struck all the beholders with horror. On the table was found a letter written by himself stating that he had ruined his wife and children and could not survive. The fact was that he had engaged in some Australian company, which was in a precarious state, threatening bankruptcy, and heavy calls had been made upon him, which he feared might ruin him and deprive his wife of her newly acquired property. The poor widow was left alone with nine children to fight her way in the world. All her husband's affairs were seized to pay his "Calls", but her fortune was not touched, as the bank did not fail. Poor Amelia died of grief two years later.

In the Autumn of this year we migrated to Leamington for the winter; our residence was in the Lower Parade, where all the gay folks rode and drove, so life was very pleasant. There were many nice Catholic families in the congregation, and we made many friends. The Chapel was not bad for that period. It had been built at the expense of the reverend Crosley,[1] who was collecting money for it in 1827 abroad. He was still living, but superannuated, at the Convent of Colletines at Baddesley Clinton. The Reverend Mr. and Mrs. Donnelle[2] was then doing duty. Soon after our arrival at Leamington, Dr. London M.D., and master of Ceremonies, called upon us; he was a most agreeable and learned man and became a great favourite. He was connected with the Napiers of Merchiston,[3] which name he bore as a Christian name, and finding that we descended from that family, he was much pleased. He procured an

---

1 Rev. Crosley - Probably a mistake for Rev. B. Crosbie (1824-1831). Rev. Mr. and Mrs.
2 Donnelle. Kelly has Rev. James McDonnell. 'Mrs' may be his mother.

3 Napiers of Merchiston (near Edinburgh) would appear to be related to those of Oxford mentioned on p. 35
John Napier Laird of Merchiston (1550-1617) was the inventor of Logarithms. He was educated at St. Andrews and in no way connected with Oxford.

engraved portrait of our common ancestor, the "Wizard of Oxford", who was the great mathematician of the University. My grandmother had a very serious illness at this time. Indeed she was seldom well. It being our duty to attend to her on those occasions, we became very experienced nurses. It would have seemed to us most unnatural that a sick-room should be left without one or other of us in attendance on the invalid. Before we left Leamington, we took various excursions to Warwick and Coventry to see the "Lions" of the town. At the latter place, we saw "Peeping Tom", who was then in all his glory at a window of a Corner house at the top story. He was a wooden figure of a man, life size, dressed in antique style. It was in the spring of 1835 that Alicia and I went to Eaton, whilst our grandparents and servant started for Baddesley Clinton. They boarded in the Priest's house for that summer, and different members of the Eaton party paid them visits. In the autumn, my father, mother, Alicia and Euphemia went with the intention of spending a week there. They set off from Eaton in the Phaeton, and my father drove. When they got about half way in the journey, they stopped to refresh the horses, and someone most imprudently removed the blinkers from the horse, which took fright, turned round and ran away, the ladies being in the carriage. After galloping at a mad rate for some time, the carriage was drawn over a heap of stones. My mother was thrown out and fell with her head on a sharp stone, which inflicted a terrible wound, and the shock caused concussion of the brain. She was taken up for dead. In the meantime, the horses went on until they ran with violence into a hedge, and my two sisters were thrown right over the hedge, the shafts were broken off, and the horse ran until it was stopped.

After the party had left Eaton, we who were left behind, amused ourselves in various ways, and after dinner we all went to "Nut"in the wood. We were returning home in the dusk of the evening, when we saw a post-chaise drive up to the door, and my poor mother was lifted out quite insensible and carried up to bed. She recovered after a long and anxious illness, my sister and I nursing her all the time.

As I had not resided with my parents for many years, I spent the following year at Eaton, as I was to leave in the autumn to be married. During this time many friends called, but I was generally laid up with colds, so was deprived of all the enjoyments, for I was often disfigured with a swollen face. It so happened, I suppose, to blunt the edge of the eagerness with which I looked forward to pleasure. Most of this summer was spent by me in preparing my wedding trousseau, most of which I made with my nimble fingers, and it was so abundant that even now, after 37 years, some articles still remain. I also read Scott's novel, studied classical authors, drew, and practiced duets with my sisters on the piano and guitar, so time passed very quickly and happily. Dear John was also busy preparing to pass his examinations in the London University, [1] and he was very successful in getting his diplomas. It was agreed that we should be united in holy wedlock on the 25th October. All our family were assembled for the occasion and all looked very happy. The Reverend Richard Boyle S. J.[2] was the Priest, and the Reverend Henry Stonehouse the Parson who performed the ceremony. Ours must have been one of the last weddings performed in both Churches, for soon after that, the law was altered, which made Catholic marriages legal; then a Registrar was present. On the night of the 24th, I retired early, and after I had departed to my own room, my dear brothers and sisters sat up most of the night to decorate our little Chapel and make arrangments for the morrow. In the morning of the 25th, I was up early and dressed in my wedding dress, consisting of white satin, trimmed with blond lace, a veil and orange flowers. Dear John wore a waistcoat which I had spent most of the summer in embroidering. The pattern was in gold bullion on black velvet. I had also embroidered a purse, which was used at the ceremony to contain the wedding money.[3] We met in the Chapel about 8 o'clock, I being attended by my four sisters as bridesmaids, all dressed in white figured poplins trimmed with swan down. My dear father gave me away, whilst my beloved mother stood near with the rest of the family. After the Nuptial Mass was over, we went down to breakfast and after that to the Protestant Church. All walked in procession two and two up to the communion table, where Mr. Stonehouse performed his part, and we all returned to the wedding feast.

Poor old Symonds, the gardener, an old and attached servant, offered a great surprise in the way of a large bouquet of white

---

[1] John Dolman attended courses in the Medical School of University College (1834-1837)

[2] Rev. Richard Boyle S. J. was p.p. of St. Francis Xavier's (1834-1837)

[3] Gold and silver coins used to be given by the bride groom to his bride with the words, "This gold and silver I thee give".

petunias, which were then considered a rare, choice flower. All passed off well. In the afternoon, I took leave of my beloved parents and all the dear relatives, never to see them all assembled together again. Then I took my farewell of my dear home, and we started that afternoon for Gloucester, stopping at the "Belle Hotel". The next morning, dear John went to Church, and returned with the Abbé Fosse, an old family friend. He was a very old venerable emigré French Priest who had resided and done missionary work for 30 years at Gloucester. He was an excellent man, quite a courtier in manner, and wore his hair powdered. After breakfast, we took leave of him, and took our seats in the Salisbury Coach, travelled all day and slept at Salisbury. The following day we visited the Cathedral and other places of interest, and then resumed our journey to Southampton and stayed at the Dolphin Hotel until the following Sunday night. In the morning we went to Mass and called on Mr. Horne the Priest, now at Spanish Place London. That evening we embarked in a steamer for Havre, and landed in time to hear a late Mass for the Feast of All Saints. We remained there three nights and I thought it a dirty, disagreeable place. Then we went to Rouen where we visited the Cathedral and Churches, and on the 5th November we reached Paris. Neither of us had the slightest idea where to go to, although many Hotels had been recommended. However, Providence took care of us. We met a very nice and agreeable old lady in the diligence, who seemed to take a fancy to us, and asked if we knew of a good place to drive to, when we stopped in Paris. She told us of a very comfortable Hotel. She accompanied us to it, and we found it all we could desire, and, as we found out afterwards, it was the only Hotel where there were the English comforts of carpets. We occupied a flat and I never was so comfortable in my life.

It was a very large house and several families resided in it. None had private servants, but the establishment waited on all, and there was a delighful old housekeeper who attended on all our wants. Everything seemed to be done by magic. Every morning, before going out, I wrote an order for dinner, which I left on my table, a bill of fare being provided. At the appointed hour all was served in style on silver plates and dishes with a man waiter. All the trouble I had was to pay the bill once a month, and a very moderate one it was.

We spent the day sight-seeing and left very few places unexplored, I need not detail my impression of this beautiful city. One can never adequately appreciate it. On Sundays and feast days we generally attended Mass and Vespers at Notre Dame and somtimes at St. Roche which was near to us.

On Christmas Eve we found out a Priest who could speak English, and we both went to confession. The next day poor John was so ill with a bad quinsy throat that he could not go to Mass. I felt as if everybody was looking at me, which made it very uncomfortable. The cold soon set in and I saw sledges for the first time on the Boulevards, and their numerous little bells made a cheerful jingle. At last we grew tired of the gay Capital, and made our way to Nantes, to the residence of Captain and Mrs. Comte, John's sister and brother-in-law. I did not enjoy this visit, because I did not like their French ways. They had two spoilt children of two and eight, and no nursery. I disliked all their habits, and longed for the end of the visit, although they were so kind and did all they could to help to amuse us. I disliked their thoroughly worldly habits, and it was difficult to observe the precepts of religion. He was like most Frenchmen of his day without any religion of any kind. A sister of his lived with them, and acted as 2nd mother to the children: an excellent woman, who never thought of herself or partook of the worldly ways of the others. She had a sudden attack of fever and became delirious, and I remember sitting by her bedside one night. At the back of the room there was a staircase and the wall was very thin. Whilst I was standing by the bedside a Frenchman with wooden shoes ran down the stairs making a prodigious noise; suddenly the invalid sprang up in bed, and cried out in an attitude of attention "Ecoutez ce papillon qui descend". There was something so ludicrous in the comparison to a butterfly, that we all burst out laughing. We often went to balls at the Préfecture and enjoyed them.

The town of Nantes is very fine and noted for its shipping, which was an amusement to us. There are many islands in that part of the river Loire. One called Andretta was the government depót for ship-building, and a cousin of Captain Comte's was the governor. Mr. Gande was his name. he was very civil to us, and got up a grand fête for us, to which we went in boats, and returned late at night. At last, we took leave of our hospitable friends and directed our course to Le Mans. From Nantes we sailed up the beautiful

Loire as far as Angers, and it was delightful indeed. I think nothing can be more enchanting than travelling in the small steamers in those lovely rivers, the Rhine and the Moselle, gliding along so smoothly with magnificent scenery on either side. Our pleasure ended at Angers. We took places on the "Diligence", which was to start at 10 o'clock p.m. for some reason. The people cheated us, and as it was pitch dark, we were huddled into a conveyance which we soon discovered not to be the Coupé of the above named coach, when four men got in, whom we found out to be pig-jobbers returning from the fair. The smell was so intolerable that I nearly fainted. As soon as daylight appeared, and I saw the lining of the carriage, a shining mass of black grease, I felt as bad as if I had been on sea. We did not reach Le Mans until 9 o'clock in the morning, but I was too poorly for many days to go to the Convent. At last we paid our visit to the Visitation Convent, and oh! how pleased dear Clementina was to see us. This was the first visit since we left her there in 1824. We put up at the Boule d'or, and remained a week. The Chaplain, Monseigneur l'Abbé Boulanger, amused us very much. He knew so little of the world or of general information, and even expressed great surprise, when we assured him that there were such things as stones in England. In after years, he turned out to be a most agreeable, intelligent and well-informed author. So much for travel and study joined with intelligence. From Le Mans we went to Tours, and saw the Cathedral, then on to Blois, where we remained several days. All our old friends were so pleased to see us. Madame Sophie de Vouvre, my old school mistress, the Bernardine Nun, was simply delighted. Upon enquiry, I heard that she had retired into private life. We had previously passed the street in which she lived, and I saw an old lady looking out of the window, little thinking it was the very person we were in seach of. However, it turned out that when she saw us pass, she said to herself "If it were possible for any of the Cox family to be at Blois, I would have taken that lady for one of them". She had not seen me since I was 12 years old. From Blois we returned to Paris, then on to Boulogne. After staying with many kind friends, we resumed our journey to London. Taking the coach from there, we started for Hereford, which we reached at about 10 o'clock the next day. I can never forget the intense joy I felt at the thought of once more seeing my beloved family. At last we arrived, having been away just 6 months. My grandparents had taken a very pretty house just outside Hereford, and their joy at seeing us again was inexpressible. They treated us quite "en grande personne", and could not do enough for us. Leaving them, we went to Eaton Bishop where my dear parents and family resided, and the spot from which I had started on my wedding day. All that summer I was very busy with the help of my dear mother and sisters in preparing for the arrival of a little stranger. My husband went to York to prepare a house. When all was settled, he returned in the beginning of August, just in time to welcome "Young delight" as she was always called. The following day, being the Feast of the Assumption, Mr. Boyle, the Priest of Hereford, came over to perfom the baptismal service. The Christening took place among all the joys and blessings of home, and the infant received the names of Mary, Helen, Alicia the first in honour of the Blessed virgin, the 2nd for me, and the 3rd for her godmother. She was a beautiful baby and much admired by everyone.

Soon after this, I journeyed to York with my sister Alicia and the nurse, my husband having gone on before to arrange for our reception. We travelled by Coach to Sheffield and then to Selby. Dear Yorkshire! to my mind, the county of all that was grand and hospitable and truly English. We arrived at York its Capital, and well I remember my feelings when our post-chaise stopped at our house, the first I could call my own. It was a large house and had long been vacant, some said on account of ghosts, but as my husband believed in nothing of that sort, he took it on a lease, and had it thoroughly done up, painted and papered, with many improvements. He went to see it before my arrival, and even he had a terrible fright. He felt and saw his bed curtains move and shake without any visible aid; but he persuaded himself that there must have been mice in his bed, and had run up his curtain, although the bed was freshly put up, and the room quite renovated. He said nothing to us about this occurrence then, and we entered the house, feeling very happy. Some time after our arrival, we all went out to a party, and when we returned at night, the first thing we heard were screams and sobs from one of the maids, who was terrified out of her senses, and then I heard for the first time, that a lady, richly attired in silk, walked up and down the great staircase, and that the maid had come in contact with her. My husband would not allow me to ask any questions for fear of encouraging the servants in idle fears, so I never heard who the lady was supposed to be. Soon after that event we were out again in the evening. I had ordered refreshments to be ready for us on our return, in the dining room. Again on our return we found one of the maids in hysterics. She was not the one who had been frightened before. She had left. It seems that she took the tray to the dining room, and there saw what terrified her so much. She just had time to run back to the kitchen, and then fainted. On one occasion my brother George came to see us. As all the rooms were occupied, I made him up a bed on the sofa in the dining room. He was a strong-minded man, but he also saw what had so appalled the maid; and he told me how bewildered he had felt, then awestruck, and described to me what he had witnessed. About three months after that, I was sitting in the dining room. My husband, sister and servants had all gone to Chapel. The nurse and baby were in the nursery quite at the top of the house. I was reading, when suddenly I heard the handle of the door rattle and turn. The door opened slowly until it was quite open, and then shut again. I cannot describe what a feeling of horror came over me, when I remembered I was all alone, and no one could have got into the house, the hall door being locked. I was overcome with fear and went up to the nursery trying to conceal my fright, as I did not wish the nurse to know. I made pretence that I had come to see the baby, and remained there until the others returned. I saw the same thing which had so frightened the maids and scared and perplexed my brother. For several years I had to sit in that room alone, almost every evening. I sometimes saw the spectre, and at other times the door handle only rattled without opening. It always gave me a great turn when it occurred. I never could account for it. It may seem strange that I selected that room in preference to any other when I was so much alone, but it was so retired and far removed from the maddening riot of the street upon which the other rooms looked, and remote from the busy hum of men that I preferred it, although at times I was terribly frightened, but I kept all this to myself, knowing that my husband did not believe in such things. Another strange thing in this house was that as soon as the family began night prayers, footsteps were heard in the room above, as if some person was walking about. Not infrequently I sent up in the middle of prayers to know who was there, but no one was ever to be seen.

We left the house in 1852, and the people who succeeded us did not remain long. Ultimately, it was divided into two houses under the great staircase. Where the lady in silk used to walk, a skeleton was found. In the mysterous dining room, the former occupant died. One day, in looking up suddenly, I distinctly saw an old woman leaning over someone in an armchair. The next instant she had disappeared. I always forced myself to believe this was an optical illusion.

Our first days were very happy ones. I entered with great spirit into my new ménage, and my husband with equal energy in pursuit of his profession, while my sister added much to our society.

Mr. Rayment* and Mr. Billington were the Priests, the latter a very zealous Priest, who died of Irish fever, which he caught while attending the poor people. The former was a brother to Mr. Rayment of Worcester, a medical man, in those days styled apothecaries; being neither surgeons nor physicians, they generally carried out the orders of the latter, but might also practise on their own account. That class of people have long ceased to exist. They were different to the Druggist and Chemist who were always considered tradesmen, but the apothecary was looked upon as a gentleman. Physicians ranked much higher than the medical men of the present day, the profession being generally followed by younger sons of the great families, or the elder sons of gentleman of moderate fortune.

About this time I heard of my dear aunt's death. When my grandfather visited her one day, he found her very unwell, so they decided to send for the Priest. Mr. Boyle, the Priest at Hereford, near which town she lived, was out, and the next clergyman was 14 miles off. He was accordingly written to, to come at once, and my father posted the letter. Just as he was doing so, he met another gentleman, who had come up for the same purpose, and recognised in him a Priest of his acquaintance, who had come up on a visit. He told him of his aunt's state. Luckily he had the holy oils in his pocket, and at once returned with my father. They found the invalid sitting by the fire in her room and when she was told of the Priest's mission, she retired to her bed, lay down and received the Sacraments. She then asked for her keys and desk, which she opened, and gave some money to the Priest for the poor, composed herself in bed, and began to pray, in doing which, she calmly breathed her last. Prayer was her habitual occupation.

* Kelly gives Benedict Rayment as incumbent from (1811-1842). His successor was Rev. Thomas Billington V.G., who died 1849.

During this winter we went to many parties and gave many in return. I fell into blunders of various kinds, which young house-keepers are apt to do. I had tact enough not to invite Catholics and Protestants to the same assembly, but this did not save me from another kind of blunder. One evening we had a large party, and I did all I could to make things go off well; but with all my efforts I did not succeed. People were silent and dull; however, before the end of the evening, I found out that several of the guests were at daggers drawn with one another, and each had considered himself offended by meeting the other. Among the rest were two middle-aged sisters; when the time came for them to go, I noticed that one brushed past the other without even saying "Goodnight". I thought this very odd, and could not understand it, so someone said "Oh! do you not know, they have never spoken to one another for years, and never meet in the same room". On another occasion, I noticed in a corner of the room that one gentleman was always left unnoticed. Everyone slighted him, and I was then told he had been in prison for swindling. He married a great friend of mine. In my inexperience I had various other troubles from servants, partly because, like most young housekeepers, I was afraid to reprimand them too often, for fear of provoking insolence. At last, after a good many changes, I succeeded in getting all I could desire, and my cook and nurse remained with us for many years, being quite devoted to me. In the month of July my sister Alicia left us for London. She was to travel by water, and John and I saw her safe on the steamer at Hull. She returned to Eaton Bishop, her home, only for a short time, as she heard that her grandmother was very ill at Hereford, and her place was in the sick room. The poor old lady was dying of cancer. She had been suffering a long time, but would not let my sister know, for fear she should shorten her visit to us. It must have been a terrible trial to Alicia, affectionate and sensitive as she was, to witness the tortures of one she loved so much and could not alleviate.

At last the end came. On the 29th of January 1839, having told Alicia that she rejoiced because I had just had a little son, and would recover quickly. As she knew nothing about this, her prediction was extraordinary. She had also foretold the day of her death, which was also fulfilled. She edified all who came near her by her great patience and resignation. She most humbly begged pardon of all the servants and others for anything she may ever have done to annoy them in any way. After this attack, she lingered for 3 months in dreadful agony, and having once more received the rites of the Church, she expired on the feast of the Holy Cross, 3rd May. She had suffered so much for her faith in her youth, being a convert, at a time of great bigotry, whilst the penal laws were still in force against Catholics, and had led such a saintly life for 50 years, that we all hoped she needed no purgatory, as her life had been a succession of illnesses, patiently borne.

But to return to ourselves: Shortly after Alicia's departure, my dear baby fell ill with measles. I nursed her through many anxious days. One night, as she lay in bed with me, her little head resting on my arm, we were all roused by a most curious noise like the roaring of the sea. We listened attentively for some time. Then my husband dressed and went out to find the cause, and came back and told me it was the noise of a tremendous hurricane. Many houses were blown down and immense trees uprooted. The house of one of our neighbours had all the windows smashed in, and they were employed in stuffing them with mattresses and saving the roof from being carried away. That was a terrific tempest, and a most anxious night, for I expected every moment to be crushed to death by the roof falling in. I can only remember one other tempest equal to this, and that I will describe presently. On the 29th of January, my first-born son came into the world. As his great grandmother foretold, he was an excellent good baby, and pronounced to be "as fair as a flower". His first night in this world was one of unspeakable anxiety to his father and myself. The terrible hurricane returned with more violence that before. Many houses were blown down, and a thick snow fell, which almost blinded the street passengers. I lay all that night in terror of being crushed by the falling of the house; and the knowledge that my infant was not baptized, was worse than the fear of death. At last a tremendous crash came, and I expected to be buried in the ruins, but it turned out to be the house next door to us. My dear husband went off to the Priest's house, to ask him to come and baptize the baby, but his reply was that a recent order from the Bishop forbade infant baptism in private houses. Therefore he refused to come without a special order. Poor John walked out immediately to Fulford, the Bishop's residence, two miles out of town, at the risk of being killed by the falling trees, which were being blown down on all sides. He represented to His Lordship the danger there was to a new-born infant to take it out in that storm, and consequently obtained an order for the Priest to come to the house to perform the sacred rite. The Priest came, and the child received the Holy Water of Regeneration under the name of Marmaduke Francis Dolman. He was Christened at the Church a month later. On the day of his birth, we received a French circular from an imposter calling himself the Duke of Normandy, who purported to be Louis 17th of France, viz the poor little Dauphin, who died during the revolution.

The circular in question was a manifesto of his rights, and he also declared himself to be the head of a new-fangled religion.The last-named statement put an end to all his followers. Before that, many old royalists rather believed in him, but after that, all abandoned him. The paper had been sent up to my room, to translate for a lady and gentleman downstairs who were actually in the house waiting for it when the baby was born.

In the spring of that year I received a most affectionate letter from my brother George, then studying in Edinborough. He expressed his regret that we could so seldom meet, and then added, "But I will pray that we may all meet once more in this world". It so happened that my two brothers should go to Eaton that spring, and escort me and the children to Hereford. I have never forgotten the kindness of those two brothers during that long journey, partly by coach, partly by rail. The railways only being in their infancy, the coach supplied in the intervals. Many young men would try to avoid the contact of a nurse and two babies, but they even took their turn in the nursing. George held his hand for many hours, as a screen, to keep the cold air off the baby. His prayer was fulfilled, for we all met at Eaton that summer, and it was the last time we were all together. My dear husband, ever unselfish and ever willing that I should take the children for an outing, remained at home to plod, deprived of his only solace after a day's work: the presence of his children.

For the last time my grandfather was with us on Michaelmass day 1839. We all dined together, and to celebrate the day in old custom, he had two geese, one placed at each end of the table, at which he presided himself. He was then in his 94th year. The year previously he broke his leg for the 3rd time, but he had quite recovered, and was walking very well. We took our leave of the good old man that night, and I never saw him again.

After this visit, we returned to York with my sister, Sarah. We spent a very pleasant winter, and many visitors called. The Reverend Mr. and Mrs. Carteney,* then chaplain of the Bar Convent, was almost a daily visitor. He was a convert, and a most agreeable man. He had been in the army, and had many interesting anecdotes to relate of his soldier days. He was one day bathing in the river Loire, when one of his comrades got out of his depth, and was drowning. Mr. McCarteney plunged in after him. He was seized by the dying man, who was pulling him down to destruction. He was obliged to strike him off. Then he caught hold of his hair and swam with him to the shore and saved him.

In the Autumn of 1840 I received a severe shock at the death of my dear brother George. I had found him looking very ill in the summer, and later on, he went again to Eaton to see the family. I heard that he had an influenza cold, but was better. On the night of the 31st, I had the following strange dream, which prepared me for the worst. I do not know what value to attribute to such dreams, but I have always found that they occur by way of preparation for some event to come. On this occasion, I dreamt that I was passing through scenes of great confusion, and that I saw assembled in one place above me, all our departed relations. George stood in the crowd. My grandmother was the most conspicuous figure. She was speaking to my father with great energy, whom I thought was dressed in black, and had his head bent down on his breast, with his face quite bathed in tears. In short, he looked like one in the deepest affliction. My grandmother was expostulating, and said, "You must make up your mind to part with your son. It is for his good". I woke and felt impressed, without knowing exactly why. The next day, being "All Saints Day", my husband went to mass early, and I went to the High Mass. After the service was over, I did not leave for some time. On my way home, Mr. McCarteney overtook me. He asked how I was, and I told him I felt a nervous presentiment about my brother. I told him that he had a cold, but was better last time I heard. So he tried to reassure me, and told me not to give way to low spirits. That day passed and the next, but in the evening of the 3rd day a letter arrived addressed to my husband. He read it,

---

* The Rev. Andrew Carteney was appointed Chaplain to the Bar Convent in August, 1839. He was an ex.Army Officer. He left the Army to train as a priest at Ushaw in 1820, being ordained four years later. 'Mrs.' Cartency may have been his mother, but was more likely his sister. At that time Mrs. (Mistress) was a title applicable either to a married or unmarried woman.

put it in his pocket and left the house. I then felt certain that George was dead. I threw myself on the sofa, and buried my head in the pillow. I felt distracted: when John returned he was accompanied by Mr. McCarteney, who came up to me and told me to be resigned to the will of God, and to prepare to make a great sacrifice. I then said, "You need not tell me any more. I know my brother is dead". The letter was from my sister Alicia. It began thus. "I trust our dear George has celebrated this glorious day in Heaven", the feast of All Saints, and then proceeded to relate all the details. He had been extremely unwell and kept his bed for some days, but the doctor who had just left his room was still in the house, congratulating my parents on his improvement. He was still speaking, when a sudden alarm made them all rush upstairs just in time to witness his death. He breathed his last as they came in. After the doctor left him, he fell into a doze, and woke up when his sister Alicia came in with his dinner. He said, "Oh! Lishey I have just had such a delightful dream. I thought myself in a most beautiful country, and I was eating the most delicious water-melons". His sister laughed, and said that she had brought him some partridge and barley water. he partook of it with relish and said it was very good. He then drank some of the barley water, and whilst he was swallowing it, a violent cough came on; he was soon exhausted, and fell back on his pillow. She saw a shadow pass over his face, as of a veil drawn slowly upwards, until he grew quite pale. All was then over; his soul was already in the presence of God. The feelings of those present may be imagined. He was the idol of his parents and beloved by all. It generally happens that when Almighty God sends great affliction to his faithful servants, he also imparts great strength and resignation, and so it was on this occasion, in spite of the great grief.

I mention here that some years before, when Alicia was recovering from a serious illness, she lay awake not being able to sleep, when suddenly she seemed to see at the foot of her bed, a coffin, and at the head of it, a lady dressed in deep mourning, with a long veil over her face. She said to herself, "How like that is to Euphemia"! She gazed at the vision for some moments, and then all disappeared. She seemed rather impressed by it, and when I went to sit by her, she told me all about it. Of course, I said that her mind was weak after her illness, and her imagination had formed this picture. She seemed satisfied, and no more was said about it.

The curious part is that George died in that room 10 years afterwards. The coffin was placed at the foot of the bed in exactly the same positon that Alicia had seen it. Before the funeral, the Catholic burial service was performed by the Priest in the room, with all the relatives standing round. Euphemia stood at the head of the coffin with a long black veil, as was predicted. Thus was verified that extraordinary instance of 2nd sight, and on the very anniversary of the day Alicia saw it 10 years before.

That night Alicia spent in prayer for the repose of his soul. She was sitting up in bed saying indulgenced prayers when she became conscious of a most sweet fragrance in the room, and she saw a vision of a bright pillar composed of innumerable sparks of fire. She understood that each spark was a blessed soul, and revolved round a centre with the greatest velocity, crying out: "Joy! Joy! Eternity! Eternity!" It was made known to her that George's soul was one of those sparks, and that he was saved. My sister Clementina, the Visitation Nun, also had a vison in which she understood that her brother had no purgatory; that his intense love of God had purified his soul. One can understand why those extraordinary favours were permitted to comfort them in their grief, as our dear brother had died without the last Sacraments. The sanctity of his life might quite warrant the idea. He used all his talents, and he was greatly gifted, for the honour and glory of God, and his zcal for the spread of Catholicity quite consumed him. His faults were those caused more by nervous irritability than malice. He was the editor of the 1st Catholic paper that had faced the bigotry of Protestants since the Reformation. It was called the "Phoenix". A convert Quaker named Lucas rose up as a rival, and started another which he called the "Tablet", and which goes on to this day. George incurred great liabilities, which increased his anxieties a hundred fold, and perhaps hastened his death, which put an end to the whole concern. This winter was passed in great gloom at Eaton, as it was at York. The following year occurred another sudden death, which was the third in the family within 11 months. This same year, my sister Alicia entered the Benedictine Priory in Staffordshire, the rest of the family going to Bath. The Bridal dress for her clothing consisted of Crimson Velvet with gold ornaments, all of which was destined to be made into a vestment for the Altar. Cardinal Wiseman preached on this occasion.

In September, my little George was born. He was a fine healthy child for some days, but was taken ill and caused me very great anxiety. It seemed impossible that he could live, but under God's providence, our good friend Dr. Goldie pulled him through. My dear husband was called to France on important business. He was deeply grieved to leave me and the baby so ill, and scarcely hoped ever to see the latter again. On his return, finding us both better, the atmosphere cleared up, but alas! not for long. It was again clouded by the intelligence of dear Euphemia's illness. She caught cold at Bath, and when the family returned to Eaton, she seldom left her room. The summer was passed in hoping against hope, until the 4th of September, being a Sunday, the day she always wished to die on, she gave up her holy and innocent spirit to God. Late in the evening after a very long and distressing agony, which lasted two days, she fell into a quiet slumber from exhaustion, and in that sleep, she died. During the agony, when all the family surrounded her bed, she begged them all to retire saying, "Do go. You prevent me being resigned to God's will". Euphemia was loved and regretted by all. She was so amiable, good, sprightly and accomplished, besides being very pretty. My great regret all during Euphemia's illness was that I could not go and see her, as I was so often ill myself. The night before I heard the news of her death, I dreamt that I was sitting in my drawing room, when suddenly the door opened and Euphemia entered. She was dressed in white satin, and had a white blonde cap on her head. She had no hair, which I thought strange, as the fashion was to wear it in a large bow at the top of the head, backed by a high comb, and this was the way that Euphemia was accustomed to wear hers. I thought she looked bright and happy, and putting her arm round my neck kissed me saying. "Oh! dear Helen, you have often wished to come and see me during my illness. Now I have come to see you". I was afterwards told that Euphemia had her hair cut off during her illness and wore a blonde cap. She was buried in white satin. My nurse, who was then staying with a friend with the baby, had the same dream on the same night, only Euphemia kissed the baby and asked the nurse to pray for her. Upon hearing of her death, my husband at once went to fetch the nurse and baby, and the little darling added much to console me by its loving ways.

Among our friends at this time was Count Atroski who used to pay very long visits. He was a Polish refugee, and got into a funny scrape after he left York. He was in London at the time the Emperor of Russia was expected, and preparations for his reception were going on. One day, the Count went into a tailor's shop to order some clothes. He saw a pair of trousers which attracted his attention, and he asked who they were for. He was told that they were for the Emperor of Russia. "Well", he replied, "I hope they will shoot him". Meaning to say, "suit him". The tailor gave information to the police that a seditious Pole was planning the death of the Emperor. Poor Atroski was seized, and placed in security. His lodgings were ransacked for papers, and everything he had was taken. After a considerable time and much annoyance, he was discharged, his references being considered satisfactory, and the mistake was explained and accepted.

About this time I again rejoined my own family, as I needed to recruit my strength which was always delicate. I was sorry to leave my dear husband and children, and I had to undertake the long journey alone. I never shall forget the awful feeling of desolation that came over me at the stations among so many people I did not know. This was the first time that I travelled alone. As soon as I got out of the train at Cheltenham, a curious incident occurred. The railway was very much below the level. There was a railing of protection along the top. As soon as I got to the platform I looked to see if anyone was there to meet me, but saw no one. I then distinctly heard my father's voice calling to me, and on looking up to the railing, distinctly saw him and my brother Richard waving their hands to me, pointing also to the staircase and directing me to go that way. I said "Yes, I am coming", and directed the porter to take my luggage, as they directed. I followed, quite expecting to meet my relatives at the top of the stairs, but there was no one to be seen. I felt much puzzled, and took a cab to drive home. When I got there, I asked for an explanation; no one had left the house. My father and brother had intended to meet me, but had mistaken the hour. They were waiting for a later train.

In 1843 we again paid a visit to Eaton, and I took a final leave of my dear mother who was failing in health. She had been pretty well from time to time, and both she and my sister Sarah accompanied us to Hereford, where we spent the day shopping and buying many pretty presents for one another. My father took a house in Hereford for the winter. By that time both my dear mother and Sarah became gradually worse, each with an affection of the lungs,

Sarah having caught cold some time before. A curious coincidence occurred on Good Friday. Sarah was in her room when the butler, who was in his pantry, heard her bell ring, and went into the kitchen to ask if anyone had answered Miss Sarah's bell. When they reached the room they found Sarah in a fainting fit at the opposite end of the room to where the bell was. Said afterwards that she had wished to ring it but had not the strength to go so far. She was very ill, and it was feared she would have died that day. The news of my mother was that she grew worse day by day. On the 16th of May, the Ascension of Our Lord, she sat up in bed holding her Missal and trying to follow the Office, but she was too weak. At 4 o'clock a.m. She was seized by a sudden fit of exhaustion and expired. My brother and sister Mary Ann were with her, but Sarah was too ill to move, and my father was confined to his bed, having seriously injured his back by falling downstairs the previous day, and thus Divine Providence seemed to arrange matters to save him the affliction of seeing his dear wife die. The Reverend Mr. Waterworth* had been sent for, and, strange to say, he was up ready dressed to obey the summons. He came just in time to give her the last rites. She was buried at Eaton. The new Church had only just been opened, and the Catholics of Hereford sent to beg that the venerable remains might rest in the Church on the way to their last resting place, so it was done: the Church was hung in black for the first time, and the solemn Requiem performed. All the shops in the town were closed when the funeral procession passed through. When it reached the boundaries of Eaton Bishop, her own parish, it stopped and the Hearse gave up the precious burden to the tenants, who bore the coffin on their shoulders as far as the graveyard, about one and a half miles. Then it was deposited in its final receptacle. There was an immense crowd assembled to pay their respects to one they dearly loved. She was always so humble, and unostentatious, that it seemed as if all that honour was paid to her as a kind of reward for her humility.

After this melancholy event, the family returned to live at Eaton, and dear Sarah, whose life had been prolonged for six weeks, went to join her dear mother. She was a wonderful zealous little soul, always assisting the poor and doing works of mercy. Her energy was such that to the last day of her illness, she occupied herself in music and drawing. In fact, the doctor two days before her

* Rev. Mr. Waterworth S. J. was George Waterworth p.p. (1842-1854).

death, forbade her to do anything that might tire. She was practising when he made his visit, but her fingers were too weak to strike the notes. Her death was very sudden at the last; she just had time to receive the last rites after a severe attack of coughing, and her pure soul departed to join her sisters in Heaven. She was 28 years old, and was supposed never to have lost her baptismal innocence. She always appeared much younger than she really was.

4th July, 1844

The remnants of this once numerous family were heart-broken by so many afflictions, so they decided to spend some months with us in Yorkshire, and soon after their arrival, we all went to Whitby. My father found so many old friends, that it quite brightened him up, but my sister Mary Ann was not at all strong, and soon fell ill of a nervous fever, caused by her constant attendance on the sick members of her family. However, much to our great joy, she recovered. Among our friends at this time were the Cliffords. Mr. George Clifford had been at school with my father at Liège, when the revolution obliged the Jesuits to flee for their lives with their pupils. After going through innumerable difficulties, and crossing over to England in fishing boats, they arrived safely in their own country. They had to perform the rest of the journey on foot. My father was a delicate boy, and being quite worn-out by privations, could not keep up with the others, and loitered behind. He passed a man who was sifting quick-lime, and unfortunately, a sudden puff of wind blew it into his eyes and nearly blinded him. He never heard if he was missed by the others, but in this condition, he started off to reach his father's house at Eaton Bishop. He looked so like a beggar without shoes, and scarcely clad, with his eyes all swollen, that when he presented himself at the paternal abode, he was not recognisable. The servant who opened the door would not believe him, saying "You are not my Master's son, he was a fair, handsome youth, not a tramp like you". At last, after great difficulty, he established his claim, and was admitted. Mr. George Clifford was more fortunate, and went all the way to Stonyhurst. When the boys first caught sight of the College, they all set off to run, and he was the first to reach it. He continued his studies there, but my father did not, and they quite lost sight of each other, and never met again until this year. I introduced the two gentlemen in my drawing room, and it was a curious coincidence for them to meet again in their old age, and they spent the evening talking over those memorable days. Upon our return home, my dear husband fell ill of brain fever. It was a dreadfully anxious time, and, although I have passed through the worst of trials, none equalled this one. A consultation was held, and the doctor's verdict was, that the brain cannot be attacked without the greatest dangers existing, and intimated how seriously ill he was. What dreary days and nights I passed by his bed side, trying to alleviate the pain and his awful thirst by iced water, in a room without a fire in the middle of Autumn, with windows and doors wide open. One day I was applying leeches to his temples, when I was told that a friend of his wanted to see me downstairs. Supposing that he called on urgent business, I answered the summons at once, and found a young medical man of his acquaintance, who had been very ill, but, hearing of my husband's illness, had actually risen from his sick bed to call and see him. No sooner had I reached the room than the poor fellow fainted, and I immediately gave him a glass of wine. He slipped off his chair and I caught him in my arms. I never felt in such an awkward position, for I could not leave him. Luckily the nurse was upstairs attending to the leeches. Presently he recovered from the faint, but the wine had gone to his head, and he insisted upon going upstairs to see the invalid. I could not prevent him, and he seated himself upon the bed and began to talk in a most exciting way to my husband, who was delirious. The consequence was that he grew much worse, and caused me many more days of anxiety. At last he was out of danger. Mr. Billington, the Priest, was in constant attendance upon him, and surprised me by giving him Holy Water to drink, and I firmly believed it did him good. Years afterwards, during his last illness, when all human remedies failed, Holy Water was the only thing that gave him any relief in the excruciating agonies of body and mind. The last effort of his life was to make the sign of the Cross with Holy Water. He also frequently asked to have Mass said, thinking it the best remedy for his ill. He was so much beloved in the Town, that the house was literally besieged with "Callers", asking after him. To add to our domestic misfortunes, I fell ill with influenza, as well as the servants and children, who were all confined to bed. I did not keep mine, but waited upon the rest with the help of a woman. By this time my husband was better, and by degrees we all followed his example, and went once more to Eaton for a change of air, thus falling into comparative happiness.

When we returned home, a mission was going on, given by the celebrated Dr. Gentili*of the order of Charity. He was an Italian, and preached with great success in England and Ireland. Both missions and foreign preachers were novelties at this time in England, and he amused the congregation many times by his Italian accent and gestures. He was a gay young barrister in his youth, but, as report said, he fell in love with a young lady who refused him, and turning away in disgust from the vanity of the world, he entered Religion. He ultimately died in Dublin after a very short illness. He was buried in a vault in the Glasneven Cemetery, which is still open. It is a circular mound with vaults all round, each having an iron-grated door. The Coffins are placed on trestles, and can be seen by looking through the bars. This is not a good plan, for after the first grief and excitement are over, the feelings naturally cool, and the vaults are neglected and the trestles give away from the damp and the whole construction goes to rack and ruin. This was the case with that of Dr. Gentili, after some years, notwithstanding the large Crucifix which was planted at the head of his coffin, the same that he always used whilst preaching. His vault was thick with cobwebs and falling to pieces - such is the end of human enthusiasm.

Our next visit was to Buxton, where my father, who was gradually ailing, had gone for his health. I had often heard how ill my sister Mary Ann looked, but the family had never told me the truth, and that she was really dying. In fact, they did not realise it themselves. On the day of my arrival I was shocked to find her so weak. She came into the room leaning upon her maid's arm, but my father did not seem to think her so bad. Indeed I had hard work to break the news to him, and beg him to have medical aid at once, for I thought the end would come quickly. After the doctor's visit, he called me to his room and said, "Well, Helen, I am glad the doctor has not such a bad opinion as you seem to have about your sister". Of course, I was very glad, but my suspicions about her state did not diminish. She had a nasty little cough which I could not mistake. However, the medical visits were repeated daily for some time, and when my father spoke to me again about her, it was to tell me that the end was not far off. She never took to her bed, and had all the fancies of a consumptive patient, wishing to change houses, which was done, and ordering new clothes which she could not

* Gentili - Fr. Aloysius, an Italian Rosminian missioner who died in 1848.

wear. At last, she determined upon a journey to Penzance. She felt certain she would recover if she could go there, so all preparations were made for the journey. I had a terrible trial to endure. My dear husband wrote begging me to return home, as my little daughter was coming home for the holidays, and they could not spare me any longer. As it was very uncertain what the journey to Penzance would do for my sister, and some thought she would recover, and she was well-attended by two devoted servants, and a beloved father and brother, I thought I was duty-bound to return home. I therefore took sorrowful leave of my last remaining sister, (the two others being Nuns), and my friend and confidante. Strange to say, neither of us shed tears. There are moments of the greatest trial when one seems endowed with extraordinary strength, and I have always found that tears are not the expression of the deepest emotions of the heart. Such a moment was this, having given her my last kiss, and left to take leave of my dear father also for the last time, I shall never forget the look of anguish on his countenance. He seemed to have a presentiment that we should never more meet in this world. He bade me in a most emphatic way to kneel down for his blessing, which he gave me in solemn words. Then I got into the conveyance, and drove off, my father waving from the window. The journey to Penzance was begun on the following day, and divided by stages, according to the strength of the invalid. But on arriving at the journey's end, Mary Ann was obliged to be carried to bed. The lodgings chosen by her brother were close to the Cemetery. He had not perceived it, but she at once exclaimed. "Oh! Richard if I die here, bury me in that beautiful spot". From that time she became delirious. The Priest was in constant attendance upon her, and her pure and gentle spirit went to rejoin her sisters. She was buried in the spot she herself had chosen. After the last sad rites were performed, my father and brother returned to Eaton to live a solitary life in the house that was once so gay and bright.

On my return to York, I longed daily to hear of the dear invalid, but as there was a regulation at this time in the post, prohibiting letters to be posted or delivered on Sundays, I had many anxious periods of waiting, the distance between Cornwall and York being very great. After this great grief I fell very ill myself, fretting for the welfare of my dear father and brother. But providence pulled me through only to bear another and greater trial. I heard that my father had a cold, and I, being ill, could not go to him. However, I told my husband that if I did not hear better news on the following day, ill or well, I must go to see him. That day was Ash Wednesday. My husband went to early Mass and I was left alone. In the mean time, the post came and brought a letter in a strange handwriting from Hereford. Being so anxious about my father, I opened it, although it was addressed to my husband, and what was my horror to find it was from Mr. Waterworth, the Priest, to say that my beloved father had died suddenly during the previous night. What could I do? I could not pray, and felt bewildered. The shock had stunned me. I paced up and down the room until my husband's return, and then handed him the letter and sat down exhausted.

My father had an influenza cold which settled in his chest. His son had gone to London on business, and he was attended by a faithful servant. The priest, Mr. Waterworth, visited him and was to take him Holy Communion the following morning. He sat up that night reading and praying. At last he went to bed and told the servant to retire, and rest, as he wanted nothing. However the latter remained in the room. After a while his Master called him to his bedside, and said, "John, if I have ever given you any scandal, I beg you to forgive me". Then he got out of bed and seemed restless, but John was at his side in a moment to help him in again, but he fell forward across the bed and died exactly in the same position and on the same bed that his son died 10 years before. He was immensely regretted in his parish, on account of his good works. The peal for his death lasted 5 hours, the tenor bell revolving on its axis 5710 times, 8 ringers were employed.

Souldern Manor, home of the Dolmans, 1852—1867

Children of Samuel Cox M.D. of Eaton Bishop (1776 - 1851) and Ann McClean (1780 - 1844)

Elizabeth Mary (Lisby)	1801 - 1828
Robert Kilbye	1802 - 1822
Clementina Maria	1803 - 1881
Alicia Mildred (Lishy)	1807 - 1862
George Duncombe	1808 - 1840
Anne Helen	1810 - 1891
Euphemia	1813 - 1842
Mary Ann	1816 - 1850
Sarah Duncombe	1817 - 1844
Victor Samuel	1819 - 1819
Richard Snead	1820 - 1899

INDEX